AIR CAMPAIGN

OPERATION
LINEBACKER II 1972

The B-52s are sent to Hanoi

T0333796

MARSHALL L. MICHEL III | ILLUSTRATED BY JIM LAURIER

OSPREY PUBLISHING
Bloomsbury Publishing Plc

Kemp House, Chawley Park, Cumnor Hill, Oxford OX2 9PH, UK
29 Earlsfort Terrace, Dublin 2, Ireland
1385 Broadway, 5th Floor, New York, NY 10018, USA
Email: info@ospreypublishing.com
www.ospreypublishing.com

OSPREY is a trademark of Osprey Publishing Ltd

First published in Great Britain in 2018
Transferred to digital print in 2023

© Osprey Publishing Ltd, 2018

A catalog record for this book is available from the British Library.

Print ISBN: 978 1 4728 2760 9
ePub: 978 1 4728 2759 3
ePDF: 978 1 4728 2758 6
XML: 978 1 4728 2757 9

Maps by www.bounford.com
3D BEVs by The Black Spot
Index by Fionbar Lyons
Typeset by PDQ Digital Media Solutions, Bungay, UK
Printed and bound in India by Replika Press Private Ltd.

24 25 26 27 28   10 9 8 7 6 5

The Woodland Trust
Osprey Publishing supports the Woodland Trust, the UK's leading woodland
conservation charity.

www.ospreypublishing.com
To find out more about our authors and books visit our website. Here you
will find extracts, author interviews, details of forthcoming events and the
option to sign-up for our newsletter.

Image acknowledgments
Front cover: Art by Jim Laurier.

Back cover: Photo courtesy of the Vietnam News Agency.

Title page: A B-52D, identifiable by its "shark's fin" high tail and black
camouflage, taxis out from its revetment at Andersen AFB, Guam, on
the first day of Linebacker II. (USAF)

CONTENTS

INTRODUCTION

I flew these missions. I was a young captain flying F-4s out of Udorn Royal Thai Air Base, Thailand in December 1972 when we stood down on December 17. We knew something was up, but most of us expected that we would be going back to Hanoi again with tactical strikes. Late that afternoon we were standing by the operations desk waiting for the schedule to be posted when Jon Baker, one of the pilots who worked in the wing headquarters, walked in with his eyes as big as saucers. He said, "It's a giant f***ing BUFF[1] escort." We all knew that the United States was going all-out for the win, and we knew we were going to be a part of history being made.

So off we went for 11 nights on an operation called *Linebacker II*. For the first four nights we watched the B-52s get shot to pieces executing a stupid, inflexible plan that we later learned had been made by planners at the Strategic Air Command (SAC) headquarters in Omaha, Nebraska, planners who had never seen a surface-to-air missile. It was only the night after Christmas that the B-52 crews were able to make their own plan, a plan that quickly overwhelmed the North Vietnamese missile crews and fulfilled the statement that Kissinger had made two months before: "peace is at hand."

I knew some of the B-52 crews, and over the next few years in Officers' Club bars met many others, and over drinks I slowly learned the real story of how badly SAC had planned the missions and why it happened. Thus I, and many others who were involved with the operation, were appalled when the Office of Air Force History published a monograph, *Linebacker II: A View From the Rock*, an inaccurate and self-aggrandizing memoir written by the Andersen B-52 wing commander, Brigadier General James R. McCarthy, and his administrative assistant during the operation, Lieutenant Colonel George B. Allison.

The monograph exonerated the SAC staff from their egregious decisions – decisions that even infuriated President Nixon – and it was clear that Brigadier General McCarthy was

---

1   Big Ugly Fat F***er – the B-52's affectionate nickname

simply trying to stay in the SAC leadership's good graces in hopes of further promotion – which, justly, he did not receive.

When the Air Force in its wisdom sent me to Harvard in 1989, I took as my project the task of finding out what really happened during *Linebacker II*, and I continued the project a few years later when I was selected as the Verville Fellow at the Smithsonian's National Air and Space Museum. The project took six interesting years to complete and included a trip to Hanoi funded by the Museum, several very interesting sessions with General Alexander Haig, National Security Advisor Henry Kissinger's assistant, and interviews, written and oral, with participants in the missions. The result was my second book, *The Eleven Days of Christmas: America's Last Vietnam Battle*.

Thanks to General Haig and the participants in the operation, the book told the real story behind the planning failures and how the U-Tapao B-52 wing commander, Brigadier General Glenn Sullivan, went directly to the SAC commander and insisted that SAC allow the wings to change their tactics. His intervention probably saved the operation but cost him his career.

While *The Eleven Days* was well received, I was not completely satisfied, for two reasons. First, although I was able to gather a good deal of information from my trip to Hanoi and incorporate it into the book, this comprised mainly written translations from government sources. What I really needed to describe the operation properly was a series of meetings with a translator to interview the North Vietnamese missile crews who fought the battle.

Secondly, *The Eleven Days* dealt with operations which were very complex on both sides; and when Walter Carroll, a friend of formidable intelligence and some military background (as well as being a regular lunch partner at the Boston Club), mentioned to me that he had found the book "a bit confusing," I realized that I needed to consider that in future works.

Fortunately, in the fall of 2017 two things happened that led to the work you are about to read. First was the exciting offer from Osprey Publishing for me to write two books about the *Linebacker* campaigns. The second was a unique conference, "Dogfight to Detente," in San Diego, CA. It was a meeting of Vietnam War fighter pilots, both American and Vietnamese, and I was able to attend. There I met two younger Vietnamese pilots, Nguyen Sy Hung and Nguyen Nam Lien, who were also historians. Both had read *The Eleven Days* and another earlier book that they particularly liked, *Clashes: Air Combat Over North Vietnam 1965-1972*. They were interested in collaborating on a book written from both sides about Vietnam War air-to-air combat and invited me to come over to Vietnam and discuss it. I agreed and asked them if, at the same time, I could meet with some of the missile crews and talk about the Christmas bombing for my *Linebacker II* Osprey book.

That is how the book started. I spent two weeks in Hanoi and Saigon researching the project and Mr Sy Hung provided me with one of the few English translations of the wonderful book by Luu Trong Lan, *Christmas Bombing: Dien Bien Phu in the Air*. That book inspired me to return to the B-52 Victory Museum in Hanoi. I had visited this museum several times before but mainly to look at the aircraft and missiles; after reading Luu Trong Lan's book I realized that the most important objects in the museum were in fact the books that were preserved in glass cases. These books described the long process the Vietnamese missile crews went through to learn how to defeat the B-52s' powerful electronic warfare suite that was intended to jam the most advanced Soviet Cold War missile systems. Luu Trong Lan described how early in the war officers from the North Vietnamese Air Defense headquarters went south where the B-52s operated regularly and painstakingly drew images of the B-52 jamming patterns as well as learning what the B-52 tactics were, the altitudes and speeds they flew, and any other relevant information. The B-52s had never been to Hanoi, so when these trips were made they probably seemed almost academic, though the North Vietnamese were able to shoot a few missiles at B-52s in Laos or in the very south of North Vietnam – missile shots that missed but made the B-52 crews (and SAC) very nervous.

An F-4D carrying the deadly laser-guided bombs that wreaked havoc on North Vietnamese point targets during the few days of good weather during *Linebacker II*. (National Museum of the USAF)

This study of the B-52s' tactics and the meticulously made drawings of jamming patterns allowed the Air Defense Command to prepare their crews for the B-52 raids in December 1972 and to impose significant losses on the American attackers. In fact, one night they forced the cancelation of one B-52 raid, something no other air force – Japanese, German, or Soviet (flying in the Korean War) – had ever been able to do.

This book will focus entirely on the nightly B-52 raids, including what led up to them, and the North Vietnamese response. The United States did fly daily tactical strike missions into the Hanoi area with F-4s carrying the deadly laser-guided bombs and A-7s, which carried a heavy bomb load and had a very accurate bombing system, but there were only two and a half days of good weather when they could operate. On the other days the strikes were made using the LORAN (long-range navigation) navigation system, which was often inaccurate, and these were basically unopposed because the North Vietnamese were saving their missiles for the B-52s, while their MiGs had little all-weather capability. The US Navy carried out strikes as well, but it would not be an exaggeration to say that, with the B-52s bombing every night, the North Vietnamese military was uninterested in the day missions.

In the end, this is a book about how American air power ended the Vietnam War – not generally but specifically, so the reader can clearly see how the events unfolded in a medium easier to visualize than the mere use of words. Military campaigns are by nature confusing, with many moving parts, and in the case of an air campaign carried out over long distances, with numbers of different types of equipment it is especially confusing. I hope this book, with its maps, pictures, diagrams, and bird's-eye views, will make this important campaign easier to grasp.

And it was important … it was the campaign that ended America's longest and most divisive overseas war.

CHRONOLOGY

1971
The United States begins to reduce forces and withdraw aircraft from South Vietnam.

Late 1971–early 1972
The US detects North Vietnamese buildup north of the Demilitarized Zone (DMZ). It launches a series of "spoiler" air strikes and begins to send more and more aircraft to the air bases in Thailand as well as 29 additional B-52Ds to Andersen AFB, Guam, in Operation *Bullet Shot* (aka "the herd shot round the world").

1972
March 30 Operation *Nguyen Hue* – the North Vietnamese begin a three-pronged attack into South Vietnam, with great initial success.

April 6–May 10 The US begins Operation *Freedom Train* – the limited bombing of North Vietnam.

April 10 First B-52 strikes take place deep into North Vietnam, against Vinh airfield.

April 13 B-52s strike Bai Thuong and Than Hoa.

April 16 Operation *Freedom Porch* – B-52s join tactical aircraft in attacks on Haiphong and Hanoi.

April 21 and 23 B-52s return to bomb Than Hoa.

May 8 President Nixon announces the mining of Haiphong harbor (Operation *Pocket Money*) and Operation *Linebacker I* begins.

May 20–22 US President Nixon and President Leonid Brezhnev of the Soviet Union meet for a summit in Moscow. Brezhnev effectively gives the United States free rein in Vietnam.

June 5 Colonel Glenn Ray Sullivan takes command of the 307th Strategic Wing (SW), B-52Ds, U-Tapao Royal Thai Navy Base (RTNB).

April–October US air strikes, especially B-52 strikes, decimate invading North Vietnamese forces; South Vietnamese retake most of the land they lost.

October 8 Kissinger and Le Duc Tho meet in Paris; Tho offers a "breakthrough" new position. He and Kissinger discuss new proposals for a cease-fire, the withdrawal of American forces, and an exchange of prisoners of war.

October 12 Both sides arrive at a draft agreement.

October 17 Nixon approves the proposed agreement.

October 18 Kissinger flies to Saigon to meet with South Vietnamese President Thieu and brief him on the agreement.

October 23 Nixon halts US bombing/mining in North Vietnam.

October 24 South Vietnamese President Thieu publicly denounces the peace agreement.

October 25 The North Vietnamese broadcast details of the peace plan, accusing the United States of "bad faith."

October 26 Kissinger says at a White House press conference, "We believe that peace is at hand."

October 31 To the dismay of the North Vietnamese, B-52s stage the heaviest raids in three months over North Vietnam south of the 20th Parallel. US troop strength in South Vietnam is reduced to 32,200.

November 1 North Vietnam announces that there will be no further peace talks in Paris until the United States signs the draft cease-fire agreement.

November 7 Nixon wins the US Presidential election with the biggest landslide in US history, but a strongly anti-Vietnam War Congress is elected. Nixon and Kissinger are convinced that when Congress returns in January 1973 it will cut funding and end the war.

November 20 Kissinger presents a list of South Vietnamese revisions to the North Vietnamese delegation in Paris. The North Vietnamese effectively reject the changes.

November 22 A B-52 is shot down over southern North Vietnam, the first B-52 combat loss of the Vietnam War.

November 23 Kissinger lays out the US options to Nixon, including a "drastic step-up of bombing."

November 25 Kissinger and Tho complete a new draft of the agreement.

November 29 The South Vietnamese reject the new agreement.

November 30 Nixon meets with the Secretary of Defense and Joint Chiefs of Staff, and instructs them to prepare for large-scale military actions. The Chiefs are reluctant. US troop strength in South Vietnam is reduced to 25,500.

December 4 Paris talks resume, but Kissinger tells Nixon the outlook is "bleak."

December 13 Paris talks recess; Kissinger tells Nixon the North Vietnamese are "stalling," and he and Tho leave Paris.

December 14 Upon his return to the US, Kissinger urges military action. The Joint Chiefs of Staff direct the Air Force to begin planning for a three-day "maximum effort" bombing campaign to begin within 72 hours.

December 16 The Paris talks formally break down with no new date for the resumption of negotiations.

December 18 Night One: 129 B-52s strike targets around Hanoi for the first time. SAC planned strikes are three waves four hours apart. Three B-52s and one F-111 are shot down, and two B-52s heavily damaged.

December 19 Night Two: 93 B-52s attack targets in the Hanoi area, with the same targets, times, and routes as the previous night. Several B-52s are damaged but none lost.

December 20 Night Three: 99 bombers are sent to Hanoi, with the same targets, times, and routes as the first two nights. North Vietnamese SA-2s down four B-52Gs and two B-52Ds, the first and third waves of the mission. The second wave is called back, the first time in history that a US bomber raid is called off for losses.

December 21 Night Four: SAC prohibits B-52Gs from missions to Hanoi; only the B-52Ds with more powerful and sophisticated electronic countermeasures (ECM) gear are allowed over Hanoi. 30 U-Tapao B-52Ds strike Hanoi; three are lost to SA-2s. A wing of the Bach Mai hospital is hit.

December 22 Night Five: B-52 attacks are shifted away from Hanoi to the Haiphong petroleum storage areas – no B-52 losses.

December 23 Night Six: B-52s again strike far away from Hanoi – no losses.

December 24–25 Night Seven, no bombing. 36-hour Christmas stand-down from 1800hrs Christmas Eve Washington time (0500hrs Hanoi time 25 December) to 0600hrs Dec 26 Washington time (1700hrs Hanoi time). SAC turns over mission planning to Eighth Air Force headquarters on Guam, which promptly revises the previously costly tactics.

December 26 Night Eight: 120 B-52s and 113 tactical aircraft escorts strike both Hanoi and Haiphong in seven separate streams, with entry and exit in multiple directions and at different altitudes. Hanoi is blanked by chaff and the North Vietnamese air defense system overwhelmed. One B-52 is shot down near Hanoi, another is damaged and crashes at U-Tapao.

December 27 Hanoi notifies Washington that it is willing to return to Paris talks January 2 without preconditions.

December 27 Night Nine: 60 B-52s repeat the pattern of 26 December. One B-52 is lost, one heavily damaged; the crew ejects over Laos and is rescued.

December 28 Night Ten: 60 B-52s attack five targets in six waves – no losses.

December 29 Night Eleven: 60 B-52s strike again – no losses.

December 30 Nixon suspends bombing north of the 20th Parallel as "technical discussions" are scheduled to resume in Paris on 2 January.

1973

January 5 Nixon tries to placate South Vietnamese President Thieu with assurance of continued assistance in the post-settlement period.

January 8–9 Kissinger and Le Duc Tho return to Paris. Agreement is struck between the US and North Vietnam, basically the same agreement that was reached in October.

January 14 Nixon sent a message to President Thieu, "I have therefore irrevocably decided to proceed to initial the agreement on 23 January 1973 … I will do so, if necessary, alone." Nixon then sent Alexander Haig to Saigon to tell Thieu the same thing.

January 27 The Paris Peace Accords are signed.

February 12–April 4 A total of 591 American prisoners of war (POW) are released and flown back to the United States.

ATTACKERS' CAPABILITIES

US air power in South East Asia, 1972

Although there were fewer US aircraft available for *Linebacker II* than for the 1965–68 *Rolling Thunder* bombing campaign (known to the Vietnamese as the "First War of Destruction"), their capability was considerably greater, notably with laser-guided bombs (LGBs; a daylight capability) and the use of chaff to protect strike flights from surface-to-air missiles (SAMs). There were both permanent squadrons and fighter squadrons sent to the theater on temporary duty (TDY). The TDY Air Force fighter squadrons were fully operational and considered well trained by Air Force standards, and most of the pilots and crews were experienced, with at least one combat tour behind them. However, these squadrons were attached to permanent wings and often got the least desirable, most dangerous missions.

A B-52G, recognizable by its short tail, lack of external wing bomb racks, and white belly camouflage, returns to Andersen from a *Linebacker II* mission. (USAF)

US Air Force aircraft

B-52D strategic bomber

In 1965 there were nearly 200,000 US soldiers in Vietnam, and as the number of ground forces increased the US Army leadership began to press to use the Strategic Air Command (SAC) B-52s for additional firepower. At first SAC tried to avoid getting B-52s involved in the conflict. The commander of SAC said, "[Vietnam] is not our [SAC's] business. We don't want to get into the business of dropping conventional bombs." Another SAC general remembered later, "There was a lot of opposition in SAC and the Air [Force] Staff to B-52s being used for conventional bombing … SAC was dragged kicking and screaming into [the Vietnam War]."

In the summer of 1965 the B-52s began to fly conventional strike missions into South Vietnam from Andersen AFB, Guam, a 12-hour flight that required at least one refueling. By late 1965 SAC realized it would have a long-term commitment to the Vietnam War, and the command modified its oldest but most numerous model of the B-52, the B-52D, with a "Big Belly" conversion for conventional bombing. The modification increased the

As part of its "Big Belly" modification for conventional warfare in Vietnam, a B-52D carried "clips" of 20 500lb bombs internally for rapid loading to bring its bomb load to 108 bombs. (National Museum of the USAF)

B-52D's internal bomb load from 27 to 84 bombs which, combined with the 24 bombs on modified underwing bomb racks (originally designed for the carrying of Hound Dog cruise missiles), gave the Ds the capability of carrying up to 108 bombs totaling 60,000lb. These B-52s began to arrive in April 1966.

To make the B-52 fleet even more effective, in the spring of 1967 the United States made an agreement with the government of Thailand that allowed B-52s to be stationed at the Royal Thai Navy Base (RTNB) at U-Tapao on the Gulf of Siam. U-Tapao – "U-T," as it was quickly dubbed – immediately showed significant advantages over Andersen, whose 12-hour-plus missions required air refueling and were wearing on the crews and aircraft. U-Tapao missions did not require inflight refueling and lasted about four and a half hours, allowing the crews and the aircraft to be used more often. The U-T B-52Ds could also carry 750lb bombs on their external racks, while Andersen B-52s could only carry 500lb bombs externally for drag reasons.

One of the biggest boosts to the bomb loads of the B-52Ds was the external bomb racks modified from the carrier of the AGM-28 Hound Dog cruise missile. These racks could carry an extra 24 bombs, 500lb Mk 82s from Andersen and 750lb M117 bombs from U-Tapao. The B-52Gs lacked these racks. (Author's collection)

A Korat RTFB F-4E. Often the Korat F-4Es were paired with a single F-105G to form a SAM site "hunter-killer" team, but while this was effective during the day it was not successful during the night B-52 missions when the SAM sites could not be seen. (Author's collection)

B-52s flew in three-ship "cells," bombing by radar from over 30,000ft, but they did not bomb with pin-point accuracy. Over Hanoi the B-52s used their own internal radar bombing system, called "synchronous bombing." This meant that each B-52 in a three-ship cell was in fact making its own bomb run, and occasionally one aircraft would break formation and downgrade the collective jamming of the cell.

A cell's bombing "box," where the cell's 324 500lb and 750lb bombs were supposed to fall, was an area about ⅝ mile wide and 2 miles long. The bombers were supposedly able to drop their bombs within 800ft of a target, but this varied with the bomb aiming system used. Over Hanoi it was about 1,200ft or even more; this reduced bombing effectiveness by half, which meant that twice as many bombers had to be sent to a target. Moreover, shortcomings in accuracy affected what targets could be selected. A 1,200ft error meant that some targets would be avoided to prevent civilian casualties; an error of only 800ft meant that targets closer to civilian neighborhoods could be chosen.

One wag noted that B-52 raids on jungle targets "made toothpick manufacturers curse their outmoded methods." But inefficient was different from ineffective, and the B-52s soon become the stuff of fearsome legends among the North Vietnamese. Flying at very high altitudes where they could not be heard, avoiding the contrail level so they could not be seen, and operating day or night meant that often the only warning a Communist unit received of a B-52 attack was when bombs started to explode. Those close to a B-52 attack agreed it was a terrifying experience, a force of nature much like an earthquake. Soon stories of the B-52s' raids permeated North Vietnam as soldiers returning from the battlefield described the awesome power of a B-52 strike to mesmerized family and friends.

At first the B-52s only bombed in South Vietnam, but soon they began to fly into Laos and occasionally into the very southern part of North Vietnam, where they were exposed to North Vietnamese SA-2s. For protection against the SA-2, B-52Ds carried a formidable array of electronic countermeasure (ECM) equipment that included ALT-22s used against the *Fan Song* track-while-scan beacon, and four ALT-28s, which could jam the SA-2's downlink jamming, while other jammers went after height-finder radars.

Despite these jamming systems, SAC was very afraid of losing a B-52 in combat, and for much of the war B-52 strikes would turn back if they received any sort of electronic indication from an SA-2 site.

B-52G strategic bomber
Beginning in April 1972 SAC deployed a later model B-52, the B-52G, to Andersen. The G had a "wet" wing, where the fuel was in the wing itself instead of in fuel tanks, and overall the structure was much lighter than that of the D. This gave the G much greater range than the D model, so the G could fly from Guam to Vietnam and back without inflight refueling, which made for shorter missions and required fewer tankers.

An F-111A at Takhli RTAFB with a full load of 24 high-drag "Snakeye" 500lb bombs waits for its crew for a night *Linebacker II* mission. (National Museum of the USAF)

However, problems soon appeared with the newly arrived G models and by combat criteria the G was much less effective than the older D. It had no external bomb racks and could carry only 27 750lb bombs instead of the 108 carried by a B-52D, so it took four cells (12 aircraft) of Gs to drop the same number of bombs that a single cell of B-52Ds could release. Additionally, the G's bomb release mechanism was prone to a malfunction that prevented the bombs from dropping. The G had a squared-off vertical stabilizer 8ft shorter than the D model's "shark" fin, and the shorter tail and a new control system made the G less stable and prone to rolling, making it harder to keep it in a straight line on a bomb run. The G's lighter structure and "wet" wing might also make the aircraft more vulnerable.

But the most serious problems were in the ECM equipment. Over half of the G models – 57 out of 98 – carried the most modern system for jamming the SA-2 missile, the ALT-22, but the other 41 carried the older ALT-6B, which was only about half as powerful. SAC claimed that tests had shown that the ALT-6B was just as effective as the ALT-22 against the *Fan Song* radar, but the Eighth Air Force leadership was unconvinced.

The EB-66 was the mainstay of the USAF's standoff electronic jamming effort. EB-66Cs and EB-66Es (shown here) operated in flights of three (if possible) to see and jam North Vietnamese early warning and intercept radars and to warn strike flights of MiG and SAM locations. These old aircraft suffered terrific maintenance problems but managed to support the entire *Linebacker II* operation. (USAF)

The F-105G Wild Weasel was the mainstay of the USAF's anti-SAM strike force. The F-105G shown here carries an AGM-45 Shrike on the outboard station of both wings and an AGM-78 Standard ARM on the inboard station, and a centerline and left outboard fuel tank. (National Museum of the USAF)

KC-135 tanker

Outside of the B-52s, the KC-135 tankers were arguably the most critical aircraft during *Linebacker II*, and it could be said the Vietnam air war would have been impossible without these tankers. The KC-135s were part of Operation *Young Tiger*, and during *Linebacker II* there were 60 KC-135s at Kadena Air Base, Okinawa, 46 at U-Tapao RTAFB, 28 at Clark AFB, Philippines, 20 at Takhli RTAFB, and seven at Korat RTAFB.

F-4 Phantom II tactical aircraft

By far the most numerous of the support aircraft was the F-4 Phantom II. The F-4E was the most modern F-4 and the first to carry an internal 20mm Vulcan cannon, making it the most effective Air Force day fighter. However, because the most important missions were flown at night, the F-4E was not as effective during *Linebacker II* as the earlier model F-4D. Ubon F-4Ds carried out the crucial chaff missions and during the day carried laser-guided bombs (LGBs) and, more importantly, the Pave Knife laser-guidance pod, which was critical to any successful LGB bombing mission. Many Udorn F-4Ds carried the APX-80 *Combat Tree*, which could identify North Vietnamese MiGs by interrogating the MiGs' transponders, allowing F-4Ds to fire their AIM-7s without visually identifying the target.

The EF-4C supplemented the F-105Gs. The EF-4C had better performance but could not carry the large and effective AGM-78 Standard ARM. (National Museum of the USAF)

F-111 strike bomber

The 474th Tactical Fighter Wing (TFW, Deployed) had three squadrons of F-111As which provided a night, all-weather strike capability to support the B-52 raids. Their most important missions were airfield attack carrying 12 high-drag "Snakeye" 500lb bombs.

EB-66 electronic warfare aircraft

At the beginning of *Linebacker I* in May 1972 the Air Force sent eight EB-66Cs and EB-66Es from Shaw AFB to Korat, and by the time *Linebacker II* began most of the EB-66s in the Air Force inventory were at Korat. The ELINT EB-66C could detect enemy electronic transmissions and jam them, identify MiG transponder and *Fan Song* signals, and provide MiG and SAM warnings. The EB-66E carried ALT-6B spot noise jammers that performed high-power barrage and tunable jamming to jam SAMs, early warning, and ground-controlled intercept radar. Both the EB-66Cs and EB-66Es were part of the 42nd Tactical

The original chaff corridors were laid by a modification of the M129E leaflet bomb, the MJU-1/B chaff bomb. Its clamshell doors were opened by a mechanical time nose fuse. (Author's collection)

Electronic Warfare Squadron (TEWS) which provided the bulk of the standoff jamming during *Linebacker II*. During the *Linebacker II* B-52 raids three EB-66s, both C and E models, orbited 40 nautical miles (nm) west of Hanoi. The EB-66s were old and plagued with maintenance problems, primarily fuel cell leaks and engine failures, and during *Linebacker II* the 42nd TEWS had 20 EB-66 airframes but only five or six sets of usable engines. Maintenance crews would rotate the engines around the airframes to try to balance the hours on the airframes, but there were almost no useable EB-66s left when *Linebacker II* ended.

F-105G Wild Weasel

"Wild Weasel" aircraft were used to attack SAM sites with anti-radiation missiles (ARMs). The latest Air Force Wild Weasel, the F-105G, had been in the combat since mid-1969

The large ALE-38 chaff dispensers used in *Linebacker II* missions had originally been carried under the wings of Firebee target drones to drop chaff and present a larger radar target for missile tests. (National Museum of the USAF)

A variety of ECM pods were carried by the B-52 escorts for protection against SAMs and radar-guided antiaircraft guns. Left is an ALQ-71 and right is an ALQ-119. (National Museum of the USAF)

and could carry the large AGM-78B Standard anti-radiation missile as well as the smaller, less effective AGM-45 Shrike. The Wild Weasels were based at Korat and during the day an F-105G was paired with two F-4Es as a hunter-killer team for visual attacks on SAM sites. This pairing proved extremely effective during *Linebacker I* but was not effective during the night missions of *Linebacker II*, when the Weasels acted mostly as a deterrent and did insignificant damage to the North Vietnamese SA-2 systems.

EF-4C Wild Weasel

The F-105Gs were augmented in October 1972 by EF-4Cs of the 67th Tactical Fighter Squadron, which came to Korat from Kadena AFB, Okinawa. The EF-4Cs had a difficult gestation before they were combat capable and had limited usefulness because they could not carry the AGM-78, but they provided a useful supplement to the F-105Gs.

However, while the Wild Weasels were improved, the North Vietnamese had also developed techniques to minimize their exposure to the ARMs carried by the Weasels.

US Navy aircraft

The US Navy had five carriers in the region, the *Enterprise, Saratoga, Oriskany, America,* and *Ranger,* and they supported *Linebacker II* missions. These carriers operated A-7E Wild Weasels which carried Shrikes and supported the B-52 operations, supplementing the Air Force Wild Weasels, and the two squadrons of the highly capable EA-6Bs flew 720 sorties during the operation, jamming from just off the coast in the Gulf of Tonkin, and were especially effective covering missions over Haiphong harbor. Unfortunately, the EA-6Bs were not allowed to fly over land because the Navy was afraid one would be lost with its advanced electronic equipment.

Electronic countermeasures

Jamming

The many jammers on the B-52 were very helpful and protected the aircraft to within 8–10nm of the SAM site. At this point, occasionally "burn through" could occur as the *Fan Song* beam overpowered the jamming signal, enabling the controller to locate a target for his missiles, though for a three-ship cell in formation with all jammers working this was very difficult. However, because of the B-52's antenna propagation pattern, jamming coverage decreased markedly during maneuvers, especially in steeply banked turns when the strongest signal might not blanket every radar that could track the target and open fire. Jamming was best employed in conjunction with chaff.

These two anti-radiation missiles (ARMs), the small AGM-45 Shrike on the outboard station and the larger AGM-78 Standard ARM, homed in on the *Fan Song* radar emissions. They were much feared by North Vietnamese missile crews, but the ARMs had limitations. The Shrike had a very small warhead and no memory circuit, so if the *Fan Song* shut down, the missile would not guide. The Standard ARM had a large warhead, longer range, and a memory circuit, but was unreliable. (National Museum of the USAF)

Chaff

Chaff was the simplest of radar countermeasures, comprising small, thin pieces of aluminum that floated in the air. Chaff had been used since World War II and was a simple but extremely effective method of jamming North Vietnamese radars.

Chaff saw limited service during *Rolling Thunder* because Air Force fighter-bombers carrying the war to the North were not equipped with chaff dispensers. The Navy was also concerned that screens dense enough to blanket North Vietnamese radar would interfere with shipboard radar controlling Navy strikes.

By 1972, the electronic countermeasures situation had changed. The Air Force had developed methods of delivering World War II vintage chaff, best described as a cloud of small, thin pieces of aluminum resembling tin foil. The chaff appeared on North Vietnamese radars as a cluster of multiple returns, rendering the radar almost useless. By the time of *Linebacker I*, chaff was considered essential for the survival of the strike force in an SA-2 environment. Chaff was dropped by Ubon-based F-4s, and its first major test was on April 15, 1972, when 17 B-52s made their first raid deep into North Vietnam to attack the Haiphong petroleum storage depot. Five four-plane flights of Ubon-based F-4s used MJU-1/B leaflet bombs packed with chaff that burst at designated altitudes with a time fuse to establish a corridor about 7nm wide, 30nm long, and about 4,000ft deep. An unfavorable wind prevented the chaff from spreading as planned, but standoff jamming by three Air Force EB-66Es and three Navy EKA-3Bs and an EA-6B, plus jamming from the B-52s, resulted in no losses. For this raid, strike planners allowed just 15 minutes for the corridor to form, but experience showed that to blossom fully the chaff had to be in the air for 20–30 minutes.

Chaff bombs were useful, but the Air Force realized it needed more chaff, and by the summer of 1972 Air Force tactical units had new chaff dispensers, the AN/ALE-38, capable of laying a long, constant corridor that was reinforced by the chaff bombs. The AN/ALE had a unique origin – it had originally been carried on target drones to make them more visible for radar detection during missile tests.

The MJU-1/B provided a corridor six times as dense as the ALE-38, but only covered a small area, so many more bombs were needed to make a corridor. The ALE-38 had excellent dispersal and six ALE-38s could make a corridor of 50nm by 60nm. This would take 50 chaff bombs from six to eight F-4s, so a combination of the two systems was best.

For *Linebacker II*, the F-4s from Ubon used these externally mounted ALE-38 chaff dispensing pods, augmented by the MJU-1/B chaff bombs that increased the depth and density of the protective screen. However, the corridors could be scattered by high winds, and the chaff corridor had the tactical disadvantage of showing the defenders the route the attackers would follow. Chaff would not only spread out horizontally (width), it would also spread out vertically (height), but gravity pulled down even the light chaff, and a chaff cloud would only last about 15 minutes, depending upon any number of variables. An obvious solution was to blanket the target area with chaff, a technique for which the dispensers were well suited, but area coverage did not emerge as the standard method of chaff usage until the latter part of *Linebacker II*.

An F-4 burdened with two self-protection pods, an ALE-38 and six chaff bombs could not climb above 36,000ft, and chaff-laying equipment reduced its speed and maneuverability as well. Against air defenses, while laying the protective screen the chaff flight itself was in danger from SAMs because the chaff aircraft received no protection from the radar reflectors billowing out behind them; indeed, the trailing chaff pointed out the dispensing planes. Against SAMs, chaff flights had to depend upon their own pods and on the Wild Weasels below them. Also, the chaff flight preceded the strike force by at least 15 minutes and presented an easy target for MiG-21s, so the chaffers needed a heavy fighter escort; but this was not an issue during the *Linebacker II* night missions.

Jamming pods

During *Linebacker*, four basic types of self-protection pod were available for tactical aircraft. The ALQ-71 and ALQ-87 were both veterans of *Rolling Thunder*, and were succeeded (but not eliminated) by the ALQ-119 and ALQ-101. During *Linebacker*, these pods performed both "normal" and "special" jamming, primarily at radar components of the SAM system.

All four pods generated a modulated noise barrage to disrupt the *Fan Song* tracking beam, while the ALQ-119 and ALQ-101 could also send a deceptive radar return which caused tracking errors. When bombarded by all three kinds of normal jamming – sustained noise, supplemented by noise modulation and deception – the *Fan Song* operator was forced to resort to optical tracking, which was immune to electronic interference but useless at night.

"Special jamming" was the name for downlink or beacon jamming, and consisted of modulated noise, broadcast on the frequency used by the SAM tracking beacon that the *Fan Song* had to capture to guide the missile. *Linebacker* fighter-bomber crews considered this "special jamming" their single most effective ECM pod technique.

AGM-45 Shrike anti-radiation missile

The AGM-45 Shrike had been used since 1964 and had been a breakthrough weapon in attacking SA-2 *Fan Song* guidance radars, but by 1972 it had lost most of its effectiveness because the North Vietnamese missile crews were aware of its shortcomings. The AGM-45 had a shorter range than the SA-2 missile and also had a very small 67lb warhead, which could knock out a radar van but not the rest of the site. Even more challenging, it required a unique attack profile, and this gave the missile men plenty of time to shut the *Fan Song* down, at which point the AGM-45 "went dumb" because it had no memory circuit. The North Vietnamese missile crews were very aware of this unique profile (see picture on page 26).

The AGM-78B had more than three times the range (50 miles), a warhead three times as large (219lb), and did not require a special attack profile (the F-105G could turn up to 180 degrees after firing); but most importantly the AGM-78B had a "memory circuit" that allowed

On the top spine of this F-4D is the "towel bar" antenna for long-range navigation (LORAN) sets used by specially equipped units for very accurate navigation to lay chaff corridors. It was not always reliable in the Hanoi area. (Tony Marshall)

it to home in on a *Fan Song* even when the radar had been shut down. However, there were major problems with carrying it on the F-105G that became clear during *Linebacker I*. As early as mid-April, the missiles, along with the adapters used in carrying them, were being expended faster than they could be replaced because the wing pylon jettison mechanisms were linked, so when an F-105G had to jettison its external tank (a common occurrence in high-threat areas), it also jettisoned the AGM-78B and, more importantly, its pylon adapter attached under the opposite wing. Additionally, production of the only type being used in combat, the B model, had stopped, making a missile shortage inevitable. When *Linebacker II* ended the Wild Weasels had only 15 AGM-78Bs on hand.

Air-to-air missiles

AIM-9D/E/J Sidewinder
The Air Force used the AIM-9E and AIM-9J heat-seeking missiles, both of which were less effective than the Navy's AIM-9D. All were of limited use at night, and because of the sparse MiG activity, very few were fired during *Linebacker II*.

AIM-7E-2 Sparrow
Both services' F-4s used the AIM-7E-2 "dogfight Sparrow," which was the only air-to-air missile that could reasonably be used at night. It was the weapon of choice for air-to-air combat in the Air Force but rarely used by the Navy.

Navigation/bombing systems
The Air Force used AN/ARN-92 LORAN-C for day or night bad weather bombing. Since the weather was mostly cloudy during *Linebacker II*, LORAN bombing, though often inaccurate due to its distance from the stations, was the only way to strike targets during the day. LORAN-capable F-4s had a "towel bar" antenna on the spine of the aircraft.

Radar control
The most important and useful control agency was *Red Crown*, a US Navy cruiser stationed in the Gulf of Tonkin. *Red Crown* used both radar and signals intelligence and also the QRC-248, similar to the *Combat Tree*, which could interrogate the transponders of the North Vietnamese MiGs' Soviet SRO-2 transponders to pass information. Air Force pilots put *Red Crown* to good use as well. The USAF had seven EC-121Ts with the QRC-248, call sign *Disco,* to pass information, but the information was rarely timely. The Air Force attempted to duplicate the success of *Red Crown* with a land based "all fusion" center called *Teaball* that began operation in late July 1972, but it was largely unsuccessful, at least partially because of poor radio communications.

DEFENDERS' CAPABILITIES
North Vietnam's missile shield

The SA-2's booster motor was highly visible for four to five seconds after it was fired which made it easy to see day or night. During *Linebacker II* the booster's flame was diffused if there was an undercast. (-/AFP/Getty Images)

The most important characteristic of the North Vietnamese defense system was its radar coverage and its integration of radar control with surface-to-air missiles (SAMs), antiaircraft guns, and MiG fighters. They were all combined in a single service, the Air Defense-Air Force Service (Air Force Branch, Missile Branch, Radar Branch, and Antiaircraft Artillery), and under a single command, the Air Defense Command. The challenge that the North Vietnamese defense system faced during *Linebacker II* was that the missions were flown day and night, and the important B-52 missions were flown at night. This eliminated MiGs from the defenses for much of the operation and put the burden of the defenses on the SAM systems which were, in the end, unable to keep up with the attacks.

Radar

The early warning system began operations in early 1964 with a few Soviet-supplied and -manned radar sets in the Hanoi area, but as American attacks increased the radar system was reinforced by the Soviets and soon covered all North Vietnam, also reaching well into Laos and into northern South Vietnam. This was no mean feat: radar sets had to be dismantled, carried by hand to high mountain tops to give better look angles, and reassembled; and once in place communication links had to be established to Air Defense Command headquarters. Additionally, a robust system of radio listening posts and visual ground observers was established. The system was fully operational and very effective for much of Operation *Rolling Thunder* (1965–68), known to the Vietnamese as the "First War of Destruction."

Throughout the war, the radar warning and control system was especially effective against USAF raids from bases in Thailand which required mass air refueling, and B-52 high-altitude raids. US Navy carrier strikes were launched from much closer to their targets and thus harder to defend against. When *Operation Rolling Thunder,* the bombing of North Vietnam, ended in late 1968, much of the northern part of the system fell into disuse, but when the American bombing campaign of North Vietnam was renewed in April 1972, the system was quickly resurrected and became fully functional again. By the end of the *Linebacker* bombing in October 1972 the system was equally effective day or night, and while it could be jammed it always retained the capability to identify a raid's incoming direction and track it, even if numbers and altitude readings were degraded.

Command and control

The Air Defense headquarters, which was located in a grotto outside of Hanoi, saw the overall picture, but after identifying a raid it left the battle to the regimental headquarters. An SA-2 regiment headquarters controlled a P-14 *Tall King* and a P-12 Yenisei *Spoon Rest* radar that gave warning of an incoming raid, as well as a *Flat Face* long-range C-band radar search and track radar and a *Side Net* height-finder. When a raid was detected the headquarters picked out a target, gave it a number, then passed the range, bearing, and altitude information from these radars down to the battalion operators and their RSN-75 *Fan Song* acquisition radar via land line to the battalions' operators to allow them to coordinate their searches. Each of the missile battalions had four vehicles. The PV van had the radar antennas and transmitter and, because anti-radiation missiles homed in on the van's radars, it was set as far away from the rest of the vehicles as possible. The UV van was about the size of a tractor-trailer, and inside was a seven-man crew – the battalion commander, a fire-control officer, three guidance officers, a plotter, and a missile technical officer. The AV van had tracking and transmitter equipment, and the RV van contained the diesel engines to provide electrical power. All the vans were connected by cables. The regiment also had a technical battalion responsible for missile assembly and maintenance and the *Fan Song* radar. The entire system, including the missiles, was portable – it could be moved – but not mobile, that is self-contained. The battalion required a fixed site to set up the cables.

The SA-2 missile was generally described by American air crews as looking like a "flying telephone pole." (Author's collection)

Surface-to-air missiles

The Soviet Union agreed to supply the North Vietnamese with air defense weapons in November 1964 after the first American air attacks, and for the rest of the war supplied MiG fighters, large numbers of antiaircraft guns and radars and, most importantly, the SA-75 *Dvina* (NATO name: SA-2F *Guideline*) SAM systems with *Fan Song* fire-control radar. In 1965 the North Vietnamese received 16 systems and one training system, in 1966 18 systems and one training system, in 1967 42 systems and two training systems, and in 1968 four systems.

After Rolling *Thunder* ended in late 1968, only two systems more were supplied in 1969 and none in 1970 and 1971, but when the 1972 bombing campaigns began a further 12 systems were provided. In 1972, because of the mining of Haiphong harbor, the systems had to be sent by rail from China, which often caused delays.

The first SAM unit, the 236th Regiment, was manned by an elite group of outstanding technical students taken from universities or technical high schools and rushed into service when the first Soviet advisors and the SAM systems arrived in April 1965. By the end of July 1965, the regiment had scored its first kill, though the attack was carried out by the Soviet advisors. The US struck back quickly and, even though the first few American air attacks on the sites suffered heavy losses, by the end of 1965 the 236th Regiment had been almost

While the SA-2's large booster rocket was highly visible, the sustainer engine was much less visible, even at night, and once in flight the SA-2 was difficult to see. (National Museum of the USAF)

wiped out. This demoralized the young missile crews, students who had been unprepared for the rigors of combat.

Ironically, the losses had important long-term positive effects. The Air Defense Command's leadership now focused on preparing these well-educated young men for combat, and the focus was not only on the stresses of war but also on mental preparation for American technological advances so they would not be intimidated. The basic idea instilled in the missile crews was that no matter what technology the Americans had, it could be overcome – failure to do so was because of *their* weaknesses and mistakes, not the American systems.

The SA-2 system

Each battalion had the *Fan Song* radar for target acquisition and missile guidance (up to three missiles at a time). The *Fan Song* system consisted of two antennas operating on different frequencies, one providing elevation (altitude) information and the other azimuth (bearing) information. The operators used the *Fan Song* to refine the *Spoon Rest* data to establish the exact position and flight path of the target and from that information calculated an intercept point. A *Fan Song* could acquire up to six targets, fire missiles at six-second intervals against a single target and guide up to three missiles. The *Fan Song* had a range of about 40 miles.

After launch, the *Fan Song* tracked both the target and the missile transponder, which had to be captured within six seconds after launch or the missile went ballistic and detonated in 60 seconds. The *Fan Song* had a narrow beam width – 7.5 x 1.5 degrees – in its scanning direction and if the missile strayed beyond the *Fan Song*'s guidance emissions – the "uplink" – it could not be guided. This narrow beam width was a weak point exploited by American "special jamming" pods which cut off the connection between the beam "uplink" and the missile transponder.

The most accurate missile guidance was provided in the "autotrack" mode once the missile uplink was established. In this mode the *Fan Song* locked on to a target and the computer rapidly generated new commands to make course corrections.

Autotrack was rarely possible in a jamming environment, which the North Vietnamese put into three categories: long-range "active jamming" from Air Force EB-66s and Navy EA-6s, close-range "active jamming from inside formation" from jamming pods, and "negative jamming," chaff, which formed a "giant wall" that blocked radar waves.

Tracking the jamming source – called "passive tracking" – enabled the North Vietnamese to diminish the effect of jamming by following the source of this noise on the operator's radar scope. Once the range was verified – often using triangulation from widely separated radar sites linked by radio or telephone – the missiles could be launched at the center of the jamming pattern. The radars were turned on just long enough to pinpoint the aircraft and a really expert *Fan Song* operator could avoid using the tracking beam and guidance signal until the SAM had risen from the launcher. Although there was considerable sacrifice of accuracy, these tactics reduced the impact of the jamming and minimized exposure to anti-radiation missiles.

The *Fan Song* operators could use a passive guidance mode, using the tracking radar to lock on the jamming signal itself and guide missiles directly towards the jamming source, known as "three-point guidance." "Three-point guidance" meant the radar, missile, and target were always lined up like three points on a straight line so the missile was always flying directly at the jamming target. Target range was estimated using charts when the target's altitude was known and was the normal method of attacking the jamming B-52s during *Linebacker II*

AL GUIDANCE AREA WITH
NG F RADAR PROB DMG
VANS & I SUPPORT VAN

I SA-2 LAUNCHER WITHOUT MISS

2 LAUNCHERS EMPTY
VEL MODE ON DOLLIES

I DST SA-2 MISSILE ON LAUNCH

-2 LAUNCHER SEVERELY DMG

I SA-2 LAUNCHER PROBABLY DMG

As seen in this picture, the SAM battalions were hard to hide from American reconnaissance because they had to keep the launchers, radar, and extra missiles fairly close together. Camouflage helped but radar emissions could lead American Wild Weasels to the sites. (Author's collection)

since the B-52s were flying at the same altitude they had been flying for many years. "Three-point guidance" meant the tracking radar could be turned off, which prevented ARMs from homing in on it, but using manual modes was difficult because it took a high degree of crew coordination and increased the missile's reaction time.

Sites and firing characteristics

In combat, each battalion had six missiles loaded on their semi-fixed, SM-63-1 single-rail launchers. Typically, another six missiles were stored on tractor-trailers near the center of the site, and a missile could be loaded from a truck in less than 20 minutes. At the beginning of the war, the batteries were positioned 200–330ft apart from each other in a hexagonal "flower" pattern, with radars and guidance systems placed in the center, but this unique "flower" shape led to the sites being easily recognizable from the air and the North Vietnamese soon discarded it for more easily hidden, if less efficient, configurations.

The SA-2 was generally described by American air crews as a "flying telephone pole," and the description of the 35ft-long missile with relatively small fins fitted well. Once launched, the SA-2's solid fuel booster rocket fired for about five to six seconds and gave out a large, highly visible plume. The booster dropped off, and the main engine fired for about 22 seconds, accelerating the missile to about Mach 3.

The warhead was a 430lb fragmentation warhead with a lethal radius of about 213ft at lower altitudes, but at higher altitudes the thinner atmosphere allowed for a wider radius of up to 820ft. The missile was relatively inaccurate with a fairly large circular error probability (CEP) for a hit, about 246ft.

The SA-2 had a 430lb fragmentation warhead that could be detonated by a proximity fuse, contact, or a command from the ground. The large warhead compensated for the missile's relative inaccuracy, over 200ft. (Author's collection)

Assembly and maintenance

The missiles were shipped in long, cylindrical containers called "cigars." When needed, the missiles were assembled by a regiment's technical battalion whose technicians examined and tested electronic and guidance systems, mounted the wings, then fueled them. Putting missiles together out of their boxes was time consuming, especially fueling, and despite the heavy pressure the North Vietnamese could only build about 40 a day.

The Soviets reduced the numbers of missiles shipped after *Rolling Thunder*, and during this period when there was no bombing and no new missiles were arriving the Hanoi missile technical battalions had extra time to work on the older missiles. The North Vietnamese put them in storage, but this was a very complicated process. First, all the missile fuel had to be removed and the fuel tanks cleaned, dried, then pressure tested. Next, all flying surfaces had to be removed, cleaned, and sealed. When *Linebacker* began, many of the missiles had been in storage for four years, and one set of missiles had been completely refurbished when it was caught in the Red River floods of 1971.

Antiaircraft artillery

The North Vietnamese also received a large number of radar-guided antiaircraft guns, the 100mm KS-19 gun, the 85mm KS-12 gun, and the S-60 57mm gun, and their SON-9/SON-9A (NATO: *Fire Can*) fire-control radars. The 100mm gun could fire 15 rounds per minute against targets up to 39,000ft. The 85mm weapon had a maximum effective range of 27,500ft and a rate of fire of between 15 and 20 rounds per minute, but in practice these large, slow-firing guns were useless against American air strikes: they could not track maneuverable fighter aircraft and in practice could not reach the B-52s. The most effective antiaircraft weapons were the radar-guided 57mm guns, which could engage a target up to 20,000ft and fired 70 rounds a minute; these were deadly to tactical aircraft when controlled by radar, but jamming pods usually prevented such radar tracking.

The main problem for the North Vietnamese was the time it took to assemble the SA-2 missiles. The missiles were shipped in cases called "cigars" and had to be removed, have the fins attached and the electronics checked, and then be transported to the regiment's technical battalion where they were fueled before they could be fired. (Vietnam News Agency)

MiGs

The Soviet Union supplied the North Vietnamese with MiG-17 fighters in February 1964, before American bombing raids began, and the 921st Sao Dao Fighter Regiment was formed at Phuc Yen (Noi Bai) Air Base, near Hanoi. From April 1965 the 921st was successful in combat, and the MiG-17s were followed by modern MiG-21s which reequipped the 921st in late 1965, while the MiG-17s moved to a new regiment, the 923rd. The MiGs were never as effective as the SAMs during *Rolling Thunder* and at one point the North Vietnamese lost so many aircraft that they had to accept a group of MiG-17 pilots from North Korea. For most of *Rolling Thunder*, MiGs waged a type of guerilla warfare against the American air forces. Later, when US jamming pods began to cut down on the effectiveness of the SAMs in mid-1967, MiG pilots aggressively stepped in to fill the gap.

During the break between *Rolling Thunder* and *Linebacker*, in March 1967, the North Vietnamese formed the 371st Air Division incorporating the 921st and 923rd Regiments. In 1969 the 925th Fighter Regiment was formed, flying the Shenyang J-6 (the Chinese-built MiG-19), and in February 1972 the North Vietnamese commissioned their fourth and last fighter regiment, the 927th Fighter Regiment, with the MiG-21PF.

From 1969 the North Vietnamese also began to try to work MiGs into the air defenses against the B-52s. After training MiG-21 pilots for night flying and using the B-52 tactics learned from the SAM regiments, in late 1971 two attempts were made to attack B-52s operating close to the Demilitarized Zone (DMZ), but they were unsuccessful.

During *Linebacker I*, despite some early losses, the 921st and 927th MiG-21s acquitted themselves well, but both the MiG-17s and MiG-19s proved inadequate and, after suffering heavy losses, were kept out of combat.

When *Linebacker II* night B-52 operations began, they exposed several major problems with the MiG force. One set of issues was simply structural – few MiG pilots were qualified for night missions, and good, night-capable airfields were limited; only Noi Bai (Phuc Yen) was a first-class airfield, the rest being simple airfields for day-only operations.

Second was the MiG-21's lack of a realistic night-combat capability. The MiG-21's RP-21 *Sapfir* radar (NATO: *Spin Scan*) was mounted in the engine's nose inlet, but the nose inlet was so narrow that only a very small radar could fit it, and the small radar had a very limited range. Also, the MiG-21s only carried R-3 *(Atoll)* heat-seeking missiles and these missiles, combined with the small radar, gave the MiG-21 very limited night capability. They would be faced with a large number of escorting American F-4s, with large radar and radar-guided AIM-7 missiles, which combined made them vastly superior to the MiGs at night. Finally, the North Vietnamese command and control system could not really identify the MiGs and keep them from being fired on by their own SAMs, and this was a problem during the day as well, since the skies were usually overcast. This combination of problems led the Air Defense Command to generally hold the MiG-21s back from attacking the B-52s after the first night, and to use them instead against the daily American tactical missions. Some MiG-21s did come up but they were harried by F-4 pilots hungry for a kill and a few were shot down. When the missile units began to run out of missiles during the last two nights, MiG-21s were sent into combat and claimed to have shot down two B-52s, including one by ramming, but no B-52s were lost on the dates the MiGs claimed the kills.

Airfields	
Phuc Yen / Noi Bai Air Base	Located approximately 19 miles north of Hanoi.
Yen Bai Air Base	Military airfield located north-northwest of Yen Bai.
Gia Lam Airport	Located in Long Bien District, on the eastern bank of the Red River.
Kep Air Base	Located near the town of Kep, Bac Giang Province, approximately 37 miles northeast of Hanoi.
Hoa Lac Air Base	Located approximately 15 miles west of Hanoi.

Countering the Americans

Anti-radiation missile (ARM) countermeasures

The AGM-45 Shrike was a relatively primitive anti-radiation missile that homed in on the *Fan Song* radar, but it was handicapped by short range, a small warhead, lack of a memory circuit and the requirement to fly a unique profile. The attacking aircraft had to be pointed at the SAM site within no more than + or – 3 degrees from the target to pick up the radar emissions, then the attacker had to pitch up to a 30-degree climb about 15 miles from the

The North Vietnamese were very familiar with the launch profile of an aircraft launching the AGM-45 Shrike, as can be seen from this diagram given to the SA-2 crews. (Author's collection)

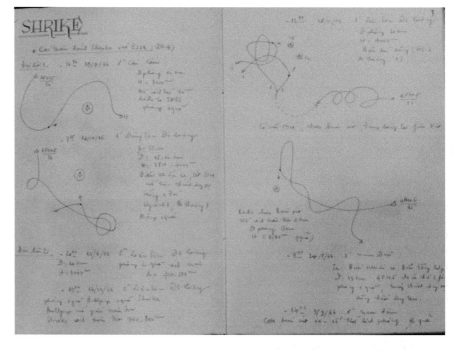

As early as 1969 the North Vietnamese were working hard on how to defeat B-52 jamming and used hand drawings to depict the different jamming patterns. This is a 1969 draft that was constantly improved to become the 1972 "Red Book." (Author's collection)

targeted *Fan Song* radar and launch the missile. The Shrike was slower than an SA-2 – a flight time of 50 seconds to the radar at max range. By the time of *Linebacker*, the North Vietnamese found the Shrike was easy to defeat if the radar controllers did not panic because it was easy for the radar controllers to tell when a Shrike was launched. Before launching, SAM crews could briefly illuminate a hostile aircraft to see if the target was equipped with a Shrike. If the aircraft began to fly the profile and fired the missile, the Shrike was neutralized with the "side-pointing techniques" – pointing the radar to the side and then turning it off briefly. The Shrike would follow the beam away from the radar and then "go dumb" and crash when it lost the signal.

The AGM-78 had a longer range, a larger warhead, and a memory circuit and could be fired from a normal flight profile, and this presented a much more difficult issue; but problems with the missile cut into its effectiveness.

To protect against ARMs during *Linebacker II*, the North Vietnamese tracked the B-52s' jamming strobes with other radars and passed the information by phone or radio to the SA-2 battalions. The SA-2 battalions waited until the B-52s were very close, then turned on the *Fan Song* radar, tracked their selected target briefly then fired. This technique minimized or entirely avoided exposure to anti-radiation missiles because of the brief time the *Fan Song* was on the air.

Countering the B-52

The B-52s were a special problem. Early on they began wreaking havoc on North Vietnamese and Viet Cong forces, and for a very long time they seemed invulnerable, flying at very high altitudes and, most importantly, attacking only in areas where there were no SA-2 missiles. Negating the B-52s became a major priority, and gradually the North Vietnamese were able to move SA-2s into southern North Vietnam close to the DMZ. To research how to combat the B-52s, a new missile regiment, the 238th, was formed at Vinh Linh, just north of the DMZ, the formal border between North and South, known to the North Vietnamese as Military Region Four.

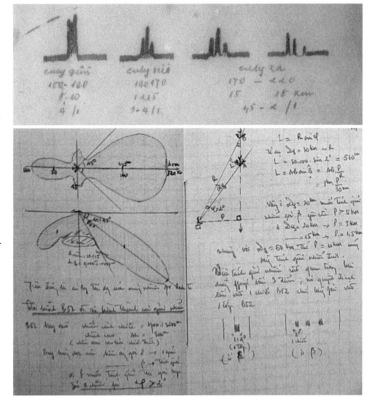

The 238th arrived at Vinh Linh in May 1967, and came under immediate attack, suffering heavy losses of men and equipment: so many that it had to consolidate its two missile battalions into one, the 84th. On September 17, 1967, the 84th fired two missiles at a cell of three B-52s. This was the first missile fired at the big bombers, but despite the battalion's claim that it shot down a B-52, no B-52s were hit, though they did divert to another target. On October 29, 1967, the 84th fired two more SA-2s at two cells of B-52s attacking targets in the DMZ, and again all missed. On January 11, 1968, four SA-2s were fired at six B-52s striking in the DMZ; all missed again but the second cell of B-52s broke off its bomb run and proceeded to its secondary target.

Two hand drawings of B-52 jamming from the 1969 draft. (Author's collection)

Since this was the first chance the North Vietnamese had to watch B-52s on SAM radar screens at first hand, the North Vietnamese Air Defense headquarters sent a team, Team B, headed by the deputy commander of the missile corps, Hoang Van Khanh, to stay with the 238th Regiment and record the action. When the bombing ceased in 1968, Team B wrote a 29-page document, "Summary of Fighting B-52s in Vinh Linh," which contained drawings of the B-52 jamming and was published in draft form in 1969. This contributed to the Hanoi–Haiphong defense plan five months later.

Linebacker I

The North Vietnamese invasion of South Vietnam in March 1972 forced the North Vietnamese to concentrate their forces and American air power took a heavy toll in what the North Vietnamese called the "Second War of Destruction," and the United States initially called Operation *Freedom Train*, then *Linebacker I*. Tactical air power with chaff corridors and laser-guided bombs was especially effective around Hanoi, though the new SA-2 optical tracking systems helped overcome the jamming. However, a far greater problem for the North Vietnamese was the massive B-52 bombing raids which decimated the basically defenseless North Vietnamese forces in South Vietnam.

The B-52s also launched, for the first time, strikes deep into North Vietnam with the full panoply of new tactics, notably chaff corridors. On April 10, 1972, B-52s attacked the airfield at Vinh and then Bai Thuong airfield on April 13. On Sunday, April 16, 17 B-52s joined tactical aircraft for raids on Hanoi and Haiphong, and on April 21 and 23 39 B-52s bombed Than Hoa again.

The North Vietnamese Air Defense Force rapidly mounted an intense effort to try to counter the big bombers. In July 1972 the General Staff had ordered the Air Defense

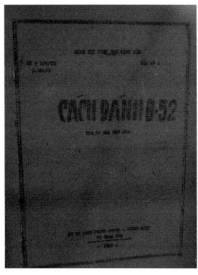

NGHỊ QUYẾT *BẤT THƯỜNG*
CỦA ĐẢNG ỦY BINH CHỦNG RA-ĐA VỀ
NHIỆM VỤ MỚI NGÀY 29/10/1972
RESOLUTION ON NEW TASKS MADE IN AN SPECIAL SESSION OF

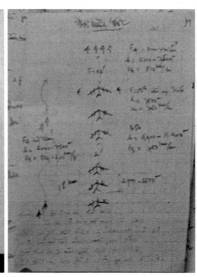

ABOVE LEFT
"The Red Book." This is the cover of the 1972 "How to Shoot Down a B-52" book that was presented to the meeting of missile men in October 1972. Ironically, at this time the Air Defense Command were moving some of their best missile regiments to Military Region Four, just north of the Demilitarized Zone (DMZ), to counter the heavy B-52 raids there. Most were not able to return in time to participate *in Linebacker II*. (Author's collection)

ABOVE CENTRE
This is the first page of the minutes of the famous "October conference" for missile crews to discuss how to shoot down B-52s. (Author's collection)

ABOVE RIGHT
One of the things that was a tremendous help to the North Vietnamese missile crews was the SAC-directed standardization of the formations, speeds, and altitudes for the B-52s during *Linebacker II*. The North Vietnamese were very familiar with these, as shown from this drawing of a B-52 cell from their 1969 draft of "How to Shoot Down a B-52." (Author's collection)

Command to increase its efforts to counter the B-52s and an elite group, Division H61, was assigned the problem. H61 built on Team B's previous research in 1967 and ordered missile crews to carefully document the B-52s' jamming patterns and to take photos of their radarscopes for further study. In September 1972 the Air Defense Command completed a plan for the defense of Hanoi against B-52 strikes, and on October 31, 1972, the Air Defense Command convened a week-long conference (to become known as the "October conference") entirely devoted to countering the B-52s. Very experienced missile officers from all levels, radar operators, controllers, missile units, and radar control stations attended.

The Deputy Chief of Air Force-Air Defense General Staff, Vu Xuan Vinh, had compiled reports on B-52 jamming from many experts, including Soviets, and from this research the Chief of Missile Operations Training Divisions, Nguyen Sinh Huy updated the 1969 "Summary of Fighting B-52s in Vinh Linh" to a new one, "Missile Arm Tactics for B-52 Combat," which, because of its red cover, became known as the "Red Book." The North Vietnamese task was made easier because SAC had standardized B-52 jamming, telling the B-52 electronic warfare officers precisely when to turn on their jammers and which radars to jam with which of the B-52's jammers. This standardized jamming gave the North Vietnamese a complete picture of the pattern of B-52 electronic warfare tactics.

After the "Red Book" was reviewed and discussed, traveling teams – nicknamed "traveling acting troupes," from the troupes of traveling actors, musicians, and singers who were part of Vietnamese culture for many centuries – went to missile units all over the country to brief them.

However, the accomplishment of producing the "Red Book" was offset when the United States stopped bombing north of 20 degrees in October 1972 and shifted the B-52 bombing to Military Region Four. The 361st Division and its two regiments, the 261st and 257th, were responsible for the Hanoi region at this time, supplemented by the 274th Regiment which was moving up from Military Region Four; but US cessation of the bombing north of 20 degrees drove the North Vietnamese to an unfortunate decision. On December 15 they decided to order the 261st, one of the best SA-2 regiments, to move away from Hanoi south to Military Region Four to counter the B-52 attacks there; this was followed on December 1 by an order to send 100 additional SA-2 missiles to the region. To compound this unfortunate decision, on December 15 the General Staff canceled the planned movement of the 267th Regiment from Military Region Four to Hanoi. The result was that Hanoi had fewer missile forces defending it than it did in 1967.

CAMPAIGN OBJECTIVES
Ending a long war

In May 1968, the United States and North Vietnam began peace talks in Paris to end the Vietnam War. The talks dragged on and on without result, while in the US domestic pressure to end the war steadily mounted. Finally, in response to this pressure, President Richard Nixon ordered the withdrawal of American ground combat forces from Vietnam in 1971 as part of a program called "Vietnamization." With the knowledge that the US would no longer fight with ground troops, in late 1971 the North Vietnamese Chief of Staff, General Nguyen Van Giap, ordered preparations for a full-scale invasion of South Vietnam. The invasion had three objectives: defeat the South Vietnamese Army, capture and hold key cities and provincial capitals, and demonstrate to the US that the South Vietnamese Army couldn't – or wouldn't – fight.

Four SAM missile regiments, the 236th, 267th, 274th, and 275th, were sent south to cover the preparations. The United States detected the buildup and tried to stop it with preemptive air strikes as well as a massive reinforcement of its Thailand-based air power, but on March 30, 1972, under cover of bad weather, 120,000 North Vietnamese troops backed by 600 tanks and artillery pieces launched the invasion, Operation *Nguyen Hue*. The attacks were initially successful and the situation on the ground rapidly became desperate, so Nixon ordered massive attacks on North Vietnam, sending in B-52 strikes for the first time, as well as calling in more Navy carriers. The United States also poured more aircraft into the combat zone, including more B-52s, the weapon the North Vietnamese feared most. In May Nixon ordered for the first time the mining of North Vietnam's main harbor, Haiphong, and began a very aggressive bombing campaign, *Linebacker* (later *Linebacker I*), against North Vietnamese targets.

These new American attacks worsened the problems Nixon was having with Congress, which was close to passing a bill that would withdraw US forces solely in exchange for American prisoners of war, leaving South Vietnam on its own. Throughout the months after the invasion President Nixon and his administration were constantly trying to stay ahead of any congressional action that might end the war prematurely.

Andersen AFB from the air. Intended for about 3,000 personnel, during *Linebacker II* it had over 12,000. (USAF)

Reinforcements after the spring 1972 North Vietnamese invasion of the South. Korat RTAFB had 72 A-7Ds added to regular aircraft for *Linebacker* and *Linebacker II*. (USAF)

To that end, Nixon took drastic action on May 8. In a nationally televised speech, he announced a major change in the US objectives for the war, stating that the United States would accept a cease-fire and would withdraw its forces from South Vietnam even if North Vietnam did not. For years the United States had demanded a complete withdrawal of North Vietnamese troops from South Vietnam, but Nixon now reduced its objectives for a peace agreement to two:

- All American prisoners of war returned.
- An internationally supervised cease-fire throughout Indochina.

Once those terms had been met, the United States would cease bombing and complete a withdrawal from Vietnam within six months.

Nixon hoped the May 8 announcement would resuscitate the Paris peace talks, but for the next four months the North Vietnamese appeared to ignore this change in the US negotiating position.

Nixon's changes to the US position did, however, play well with Hanoi's allies. From May 20–22 Nixon visited Moscow for a summit with Soviet president Leonid Brezhnev and Brezhnev, seemingly desirous of continuing to improve relations, in an exercise of *realpolitik* said in effect whatever the United States needed to do to end the war would be fine.

F-111s were part of the reinforcements at Takhli RTAFB, where they were temporarily joined by F-4Ds. (USAF)

However, while the stalemate in Paris continued, the war turned in favor of the Americans and South Vietnamese. The invasion forced the North Vietnamese Army to mass their forces, and these proved terribly vulnerable to the US bombing campaign, led by the B-52s. Taking advantage of the decimation of the North Vietnamese forces, the South Vietnamese Army recaptured most of the territory it had lost and by August controlled all 44 provincial capitals.

In Paris, US National Security Adviser Dr Henry Kissinger sensed that the more the North Vietnamese Army suffered, the more willing Le Duc Tho, North Vietnam's chief negotiator in Paris, seemed to be to talk seriously. The military successes, Nixon and Kissinger hoped, might let them negotiate an agreement before the Presidential election in November.

Then, on October 8, Tho surprised Kissinger with a new North Vietnamese position. Since the formal United States–North Vietnamese peace talks had begun in 1968, Hanoi had insisted that a precondition for any cease-fire was the replacement of the South Vietnamese government; now Tho stated that Hanoi would accept the continuation of the South Vietnamese government after a cease-fire. Two other North Vietnamese concessions were equally dramatic: Hanoi agreed to allow the United States to continue to provide military support to South Vietnam, and the North Vietnamese dropped their earlier insistence that US POWs would be released only in return for the release of communist political prisoners in South Vietnamese jails. It was clear that the North Vietnamese – while never losing sight of their main objective, the removal of all foreigners and their "lackeys" (the French-speaking Catholic elites in South Vietnam) – were willing to accept short-term objectives in expectations of a long-term victory.

In effect, North Vietnam agreed to all of the conditions spelled out by President Nixon in his May 8 speech, and Kissinger later wrote that the enormous breakthrough on October 8 was one of the greatest moments of his diplomatic career.

The two sides now began days of intense negotiation, and on October 12, they reached a draft agreement, which they agreed to sign on October 31. The key points were as follows:

- There would be a cease-fire in South Vietnam and an end to US bombing 24 hours after signing the agreement.
- The United States would withdraw its forces from South Vietnam within two months of the signing.
- The United States would replace South Vietnamese military equipment on a piece-by-piece basis.
- The United States would provide aid to North Vietnam.
- Self-determination of the government in South Vietnam was granted.
- There would not be a coalition government between North and South, but rather a National Council of National Reconciliation and Concord to act as an intermediary between the parties.
- There would be cease-fires and troop withdrawals from Laos and Cambodia.
- A group called the Formation of the International Commission of Control and Supervision would monitor the implementation of the agreement.

With an agreement that met the objectives of both the United States and the North Vietnamese, Kissinger recommended that Nixon stop the bombing of North Vietnam. On October 18, Kissinger flew to Saigon and met with President Thieu, advising him that this was the best deal that the United States and South Vietnam could achieve, based on the low level of American domestic support for the war. It was in South Vietnam's best interest to accept the agreement, and if there were any violations President Nixon would react strongly.

The following day President Thieu bluntly told Kissinger he could not accept the agreement, mainly because it allowed the continued presence of North Vietnamese troops in South Vietnam. Two days later, Thieu made his disputes with the United States public in his "State of the Nation" address to the South Vietnamese National Assembly. Although he made no mention of the Nixon proposals, he announced that peace could not come from Paris but only from victory on the battlefield, and that he would never accept a coalition government with Hanoi.

Kissinger was still in Saigon and was appalled by Thieu's response. His cable to Nixon describing the situation shows his frustration: "His [Thieu's] demands verge on insanity … He is totally oblivious to the scope of the North Vietnamese concessions [and] the ramifications of his refusal."

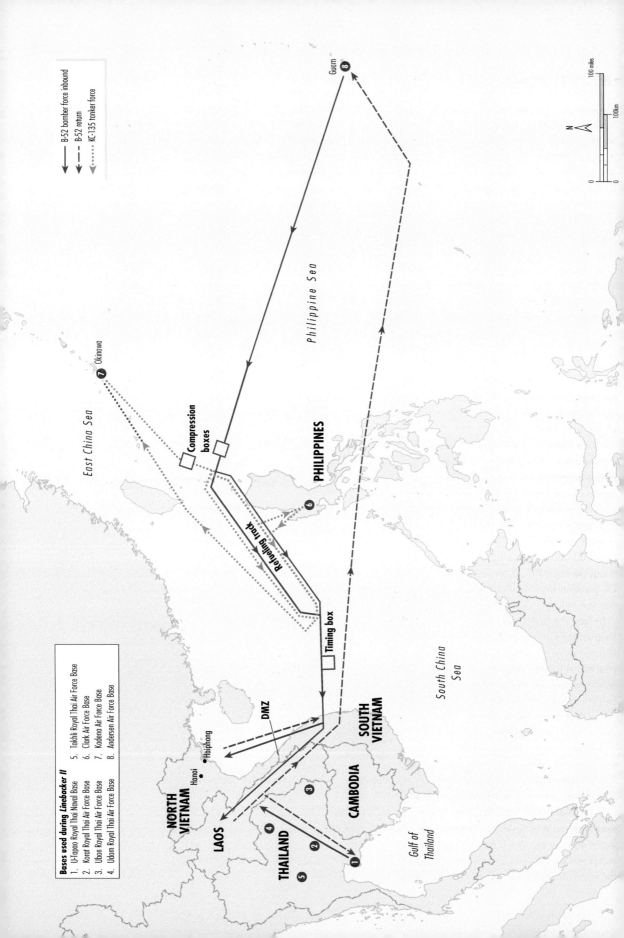

Bases used during *Linebacker II*

1. U-Tapao Royal Thai Naval Base
2. Korat Royal Thai Air Force Base
3. Ubon Royal Thai Air Force Base
4. Udorn Royal Thai Air Force Base
5. Takhli Royal Thai Air Force Base
6. Clark Air Force Base
7. Kadena Air Force Base
8. Andersen Air Force Base

→ B-52 bomber force inbound
-- → B-52 return
·····► KC-135 tanker force

Guam

Okinawa

Compression boxes

Philippine Sea

PHILIPPINES

Refueling track

East China Sea

Timing box

DMZ

Haiphong

Hanoi

NORTH VIETNAM

LAOS

THAILAND

CAMBODIA

SOUTH VIETNAM

South China Sea

Gulf of Thailand

N

100 miles

100km

OPPOSITE *LINEBACKER II* BASES AND ROUTES

By December 1972 most US Air Force (USAF) aircraft were gone from South Vietnam and were based at five Royal Thai Air Force bases (RTAFB) in Thailand.

Missions to the Hanoi area were complex, and each Thai base was responsible for a component of the missions.

Korat RTAFB had most of the responsibility for electronic warfare. Large EB-66Cs and Es provided standoff jamming, while F-105Gs and EF-4Cs attacked the missile sites with antiradiation missiles (ARMs). The ARM carriers were supported by F-4Es carrying cluster bombs for follow up attacks. Korat also was the home of the A-7Ds, day-only light attack aircraft each of which carried a heavy bomb load with a very accurate delivery system.

Ubon RTAFB had four F-4D squadrons with responsibility for dropping laser-guided bombs and chaff and other missions that required LORAN navigation.

Udorn RTAFB was the specialized air-to-air base with F-4Ds equipped with *Combat Tree,* a device that could read the North Vietnamese MiGs' transponder signals.

Takhli RTAFB had closed in October 1971 but reopened in March 1972 to support the *Linebacker* operations. The base had three squadrons of F-111As for night attack.

The B-52s were based at Andersen AFB, Guam, and U-Tapao Royal Thai Navy Base (RTNB) in Sattahip, Thailand.

Still, on October 23 Nixon reluctantly ordered a bombing halt around Hanoi but, at the same time, he increased the number of B-52s strikes into the very southern part of North Vietnam. This was intended not only to keep the pressure on the North Vietnamese but also to demonstrate to President Thieu that the US was not backing down from its support of South Vietnam.

Given Thieu's objections and in an effort to buy time to persuade Saigon without losing the agreement, Kissinger requested a delay from the North Vietnamese. Hanoi reacted badly to this request, and on October 25 the North Vietnamese government broadcast the major points of the agreement over Radio Hanoi, accusing the US government of bad faith by now attempting to delay it. This put added pressure on Nixon and Kissinger since it now appeared – accurately – that only the South Vietnamese were holding up an agreement.

With the talks on the verge of collapse and with both Hanoi and Saigon accusing the Nixon administration of duplicity, Nixon asked Kissinger, for the first time, to speak publicly about the negotiations. At an October 26 news conference, Kissinger not only explained the US position but also asserted that, although the agreement needed "clarifications," "peace was at hand," despite the statements from Hanoi and Saigon.

In fact, the agreement was dead. Nixon decided not to risk an argument with the South Vietnamese just before the US Presidential election, so he let the October 31 deadline pass without signing the agreement. He also tried to reassure Thieu by ordering an increase in weapons shipments to South Vietnam, instructing that the B-52 strikes should be moved slowly north from the DMZ and increased in intensity. He then told Kissinger to return to Paris to pressure Hanoi for a few – mainly cosmetic – changes.

But the refusal to sign the agreement on October 31 and the movement north of the B-52 strikes, changing a line set when the agreement was settled in early October, made the North Vietnamese – with justification – feel betrayed. Also fueling the North Vietnamese anger was the fact that just prior to October 31 many Viet Cong units had come out of hiding in South Vietnam to try to lay claims to territory in anticipation of the October 31 cease-fire. When there was no cease-fire the South Vietnamese forces decimated them.

In the November election Nixon won a huge victory, but there was a major downside in the Congressional elections. The anti-war members of the Senate increased to a majority; it was now certain that Congress would stop funding the war when it returned in January, and it was doubtful whether Nixon could persuade the new Congress to continue funding the war if the peace talks were not successful.

Andersen with its B-52s in their revetments. (USAF)

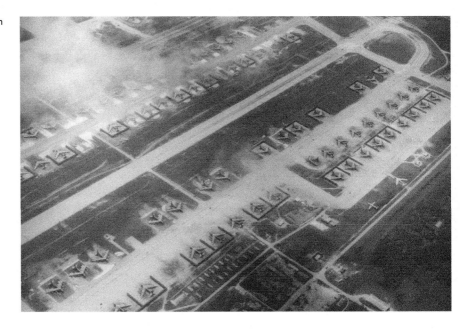

Nixon sent a message on the subject to Kissinger:

> The result of [a] check indicates that [these Senators, men who have loyally supported us] were not only unanimous but vehement in stating their conclusions that if Saigon is the only roadblock for reaching an agreement ... they will personally lead the fight when the new Congress reconvenes ... to cut off all military and economic assistance to Saigon ... under such circumstances we have no choice but to go it alone and make a separate deal with North Vietnam for the return of our POWs and for our withdrawal.

By late November it was clear to Kissinger in Paris that the North Vietnamese were beginning to have second thoughts about the agreement as they started to realize that if they simply waited the United States would be forced to leave. Time was running out for Nixon and his team – somehow a peace agreement had to be completed and Thieu convinced to sign it before Congress returned in mid-January and cut off funding for the war.

At that point, Kissinger became the first to suggest that the United States would have to resort to a military response to force the issue, telling the President:

> If the negotiations break down ... we will have to resume massive bombing and take the position that our only objective henceforth will be U.S. military disengagement in return for the release of our prisoners ... we have proven it is impossible to negotiate a more comprehensive settlement because of the implacability of the two Vietnamese sides.

Nixon accepted this but wanted to pursue a two-track approach, so the negotiations were not completely abandoned. Meanwhile, Nixon declared that if the North Vietnamese backtracked and insisted on an agreement that was worse for the United States than what had been achieved on October 12, then he would authorize massive bombing raids on North Vietnam.

On November 25, Kissinger and Tho completed a new draft of the October agreement that differed in a few respects from their October 12 agreement. At that point, Kissinger asked for a one-week recess to see whether Saigon could be persuaded to accept the agreement.

This hope came to nothing because of South Vietnamese intransigence. On November 29, the Washington-based Special Advisor to South Vietnamese President Thieu, Nguyen Phu Duc, met with President Nixon and advised him that President Thieu would not sign any agreement unless it included the promise that North Vietnam would withdraw all its troops from South Vietnam.

This was a non-starter. Since May 8 Nixon had refused to support South Vietnam's demand for a total withdrawal of North Vietnamese troops, and this meeting with Thieu's representative was a turning point for Nixon, as it was now clear that the United States and South Vietnam had different objectives. Frustrated by the intransigence of both the North and South Vietnamese, on November 30 Nixon met with Secretary of State William Rodgers, Secretary of Defense Melvin Laird, and Admiral Thomas Moorer, the Chairman of the Joint Chiefs of Staff, and told them that he wanted the military to begin planning for B-52s strikes against Hanoi.

The group resisted. Rodgers and Laird opposed the bombing on domestic political grounds, and neither Laird nor Moorer was in favor of the raids for military reasons. They did not believe that increased military action would help and Moorer added that the Air Force had advised him that B-52 raids deep into North Vietnam would result in losses, and that the Soviets would use the downed aircraft to make a full assessment of the B-52's capabilities and vulnerabilities. But the President made sure the attendees understood his intentions, and when Moorer left the meeting he alerted General John C. "J. C." Meyer at the SAC (which owned the B-52s), and then called the commanders in the Pacific and told them to be prepared for the breakdown of cease-fire negotiations and to develop a plan for an integrated and sustained air campaign against North Vietnam led by B-52s.

On December 4 Kissinger returned to Paris in a futile attempt to resume the negotiations. On the first day of meetings the North Vietnamese told him they were withdrawing the concessions they had made earlier and added new conditions that would take effect if the original October 12 agreement was not signed. Kissinger cabled President Nixon that the outlook for an acceptable settlement was bleak and recommended that Nixon address the nation in a televised speech explaining that the United States would have to resume bombing because negotiations had failed. The President refused to appear on television to announce a new bombing campaign; he then told Kissinger to make sure the record showed that, if there was a breakdown, the fault was on the North Vietnamese side. After that, the United States would let its actions speak rather than words.

Two days later, on December 6, Tho told Kissinger that North Vietnam was willing to continue the war rather than yield on the new points. Kissinger realized that the North Vietnamese were giving just enough to keep the talks going until Congress intervened, and it was clear that the two sides had reached an impasse. Kissinger cabled the President that if the negotiations broke down the next day the United States would have to resume massive bombing to secure the release of the American POWs, but Nixon let the talks continue and kept Kissinger in Paris, while leaving in place his instructions to the military to begin planning a bombing campaign. Then, chillingly, the North Vietnamese hinted to Kissinger that they might not even agree to the release of the American POWs, the main American objective. On December 13 this round of talks finally broke down and both Kissinger and Tho left Paris, leaving their deputies behind.

Both sides blamed each other for the impasse. On December 14 Kissinger gave President Nixon a point-by-point recounting of the November and December negotiations and his growing frustration with Vietnamese – North and South – duplicity. Kissinger was convinced the talks were finished without a change in the situation on the ground in Vietnam and, joined by his deputy General Alexander Haig, advocated a B-52 bombing campaign against North Vietnam for six months. Haig had been a battalion commander in Vietnam and his experience with the destructive power of the B-52s made him agree that they would be just the things to move the intransigent North Vietnamese.

Although the talks were scheduled to resume after the New Year, Nixon realized he had to act. He agreed that bombing North Vietnam was the best option to get around this impasse, but thought Kissinger unrealistic in thinking Congress would fund a six-month bombing assault on the North. The priority of the new Congress would be extricating the United States from Vietnam, and any bombing would have to be done and the issue settled before they came back into session in January.

Nixon said later that the decision to send in the B-52s was the loneliest one he ever took, but some of his later comments suggest that it was not a decision that he had difficulty making. Nixon had only three weeks to force the North Vietnamese back to the peace table to sign the October agreement and show the Thieu regime that the United States could protect South Vietnam; and a successful B-52 blitz of Hanoi appeared to be the only hope. At this point Nixon seemed to believe that the North Vietnamese respected nothing but force and therefore were contemptuous of the United States. He had already made up his mind to use the B-52s, reasoning that the level of criticism would be the same regardless of whether he used B-52s or fighters. Using the B-52s against Hanoi would be such a quantum leap in force it would show the North Vietnamese that the United States was serious and would be much more likely to lead to a quick resolution. The very fact that the B-52s were an important part of America's nuclear force added to their effect, and Nixon's willingness to risk them over Hanoi would display America's determination not only to the North Vietnamese and their Soviet and Chinese allies, but also to the Thieu regime. Here Haig had made a critical point: the B-52s could strike in bad weather, and with only a brief time available before Congress returned, the United States could not afford to wait for good weather. Nixon was certain that if he could get a peace agreement that met US objectives Congress would abide by it. In the end, the bombing was planned to be simply a part of the negotiating process – "politics by other means."

But sending the big bombers had significant risks. All the B-52s had a nuclear commitment and B-52 production lines had long since closed, so any B-52 losses would diminish America's strategic nuclear force. Losses would also produce more POWs and there was always the chance that some of the B-52 bombs would go astray. The raids would also certainly provoke a huge international outcry and large domestic protests.

Still, Nixon felt the alternatives were much worse. He was sure that Congress would cut funds for the war when they returned in January and thus end America's participation in the war. If this happened before a peace agreement, the fall of South Vietnam was inevitable, and the US POWs would remain in Hanoi, where they were certain to be used as bargaining chips. It would continue the long, humiliating nightmare, with uncertain results throughout Asia and the world.

To make sure the military understood what he wanted, Nixon followed up with further instructions:

> The strike plan … must be so configured as to create the most massive shock effect in a psychological contest. There is to be no dissipation of effort … but rather a clear concentration of effort against essential national assets designed to achieve psychological as well as physical results … B-52s should be employed in the Hanoi area as close as can reasonably be risked … we cannot allow military considerations such as long-term interdiction, etc. to dominate the targeting philosophy. Attacks … must be massive and brutal in character.

The issue was settled. On the afternoon of December 14, Nixon told Admiral Moorer to begin the bombing campaign on December 17 using the outline of the earlier plans, with B-52s hitting the targets deep in North Vietnam, especially around Hanoi. Nixon did not want military considerations to dominate – he wanted the strikes to have a psychological as well as a military effect. Nixon approved an initial three-day campaign but emphasized that the military should be prepared to extend the bombing longer. Moreover, he did not stop at simply approving the plan. Still concerned that the military might use half-measures, he issued Moorer a blunt warning:

> In the past … our political objectives have not been achieved because of too much caution on the military side … This is your chance to use military power effectively to win this war and if you don't I'll consider you personally responsible … [and] … I don't want any more of this crap about the fact that [the Air Force] couldn't hit this target or that one.

A North Vietnamese missile crew pose by their SA-2. The missile crews were highly regarded as the backbone of the North Vietnamese air defenses. (Vietnam News Agency)

After the meeting Moorer called General Meyer at SAC headquarters in Omaha, Nebraska, and told Meyer to send him a proposed list of North Vietnamese targets. The only restrictions on targets were to "minimize the danger to civilian population to the extent feasible without compromising effectiveness" and to "avoid known POW compounds, hospitals, and religious structures." The Joint Chiefs of Staff and Secretary of Defense Laird would approve targets from this SAC list and send them back to SAC to form an approved target list that SAC could choose from. The campaign was to be called *Linebacker II*.

Militarily, two things could foil Nixon's plan – heavy North Vietnamese civilian casualties or heavy US B-52 losses. Civilian casualties could be avoided by not bombing the center of Hanoi, but heavy US B-52 losses could also destroy Nixon's plan. There was a definite link between US losses and the American people's willingness to continue the war, and both Nixon and the North Vietnamese knew that if North Vietnam could inflict significant casualties on the B-52 force, it might both demoralize the United States and stiffen the North Vietnamese will to resist until Congress returned.

But heavy B-52 losses seemed unlikely. The SA-2 SAM was the only real threat to the B-52s, and since the B-52s were designed to penetrate the Soviet Union and their advanced defense system, they would surely be able to easily overpower the defenses of a Third World country.

Additionally, by late 1972 US aircrews knew how to counter the North Vietnamese defenses. The fighter-bombers of Seventh Air Force had only lost one fighter-bomber to SA-2s while bombing the Hanoi area regularly from April 1972 until the end of October 1972. Nixon and his staff were expecting SAC to conduct a skillful, thoughtful campaign; they expected losses but they can be pardoned if they anticipated that the operation would, from a military point of view, be well planned and executed. They were to be seriously disappointed.

The next day, December 15, President Nixon received his first briefing on the strikes and found out that SAC would control the B-52s from Omaha instead of passing control to the combat theater. He remembered later, "I was appalled to find that the planes had to be borrowed from different commands, involving complicated logistics and large amounts of red tape."

THE CAMPAIGN
"Maximum effort, maximum effort"

With their shipping plugs replaced by fuses, these bombs are ready to load onto a B-52 at Andersen AFB for *Linebacker II*. (USAF)

As soon as General Meyer, the SAC commander, was notified that the B-52 raids on Hanoi had been approved, he made the critical decision that all the missions would be planned in Omaha rather than in the combat zone. He passed the word to the SAC staff, and just before midnight on December 14 in Omaha – the afternoon of December 15 on Guam – the Eighth Air Force commander, General Gerald W. Johnson, was notified about the raids. Johnson was also told that the most critical part of the missions – the portion into and out of the heavily defended areas around Hanoi – would be planned by SAC headquarters in Omaha rather than by his Eighth Air Force staff at Andersen. Eighth Air Force would only be responsible for coordinating SAC's plan with the tactical units.

Johnson had been in SAC for many years and knew SAC's commitment to centralized planning, but he and his staff were still surprised. The mission planning would require a long, complex and continuous cycle of events and there were numerous reasons why the missions should not be planned at SAC headquarters, the most obvious being its distance from the combat zone. Omaha was half a world away, and the SAC staff would have to complete their mission planning 42 hours in advance of each mission so Eighth Air Force could fold it into the overall plan and send it on to the other units participating in the operation. The time differences would also considerably increase coordination problems and meant that there would be no feedback from the crews about what changes should be made. It should be noted that at this time communication was exponentially more difficult than today, since there was only a relatively small number of phone lines cleared for classified information and written material had to be sent by teletype.

SAC had always been afraid of losing a B-52 in combat, and earlier in the war had given B-52 crews orders that "no [Vietnam War] combat mission was important enough for a crew to … risk the loss of the [B-52]" and that the crews were to "break off or divert a mission if the anticipated or encountered threat became severe." However, SAC had been forced to rescind this order after protests from the American high command in Saigon; so all missions into North Vietnam were now to "press on" even in the face of SAM defenses. Eighth Air Force and the other units in the combat theater knew that the defenses around Hanoi were orders of magnitude greater than the defenses the B-52s had faced before, and intelligence reports indicated the North Vietnamese had improved their defenses against the B-52. On November 5 the North Vietnamese 263rd Regiment's two battalions, the 43rd and 44th, had heavily damaged a B-52 with SA-2s; then, on the night of November 22, another B-52, Olive 01, had been hit by two 263rd SA-2s just after it dropped its bombs. The B-52 made it to Thailand where the crew bailed out.

It was the first B-52 loss after more than seven years of combat and 112,000 B-52 missions, and Eighth Air Force staff looked carefully at what happened. The staff discovered that the chaff corridor had been blown off by high winds so that Olive 01 was outside of it, and it appeared that, even with its ECM systems, a B-52 outside of a chaff corridor was very vulnerable. The Eighth staff also noted that the B-52s had been using the same tactics – airspeeds, altitudes, jamming patterns, formations – since 1967, and they were sure that the North Vietnamese defenders were using these stereotyped patterns to help them fire their missiles. The B-52s hit in November had been struck by missiles from a single SAM site with little command and control or support from other radars, while the Hanoi area had at least nine missile sites supported by an interlocking system of radars and very effective, if somewhat archaic, command and control.

There were also operational reasons for their dismay with the idea that SAC would plan the missions. Eighth Air Force was collocated with the bulk of the B-52 force, so feedback from the crews would be rapid and changes could be made quickly. The Eighth staff had been planning B-52 missions over Vietnam for years and had developed a plan for attacks on the Hanoi area that they had forwarded to SAC in September 1972 (which SAC had ignored).

But SAC headquarters disregarded these potential problems. SAC had been ordered to fly the most important missions of the war, and critical missions had always been planned at SAC headquarters. Passing an important mission down to a subordinate unit to plan was simply not the SAC way. Flexibility and feedback from the crews had never been considered before, and they would not be considered now.

While many at SAC had known the time might come when the B-52s would be sent to bomb Hanoi, SAC's Directorate of Operations – the part of the SAC staff that was responsible for the B-52s' routing and tactics – had not developed a plan to penetrate North Vietnamese defenses. A plan had to be quickly thrown together, and because of the short time to plan the missions, the Operations Directorate decided to avoid confusing the B-52 crews. The B-52s would therefore fly the same altitudes, airspeeds, maneuvers and use the same jamming techniques they had been using since 1967. The North Vietnamese were very familiar with these stereotyped flight paths, maneuvers and jamming techniques, and SAC's inflexibility would haunt the early part of the operation.

The Directorate of Operations made another assumption: mid-air collisions would be more dangerous to the B-52s than the North Vietnamese defenses. The best way to avoid collisions, the Operations staff decided, was to send the bombers in to the Hanoi area in single file, one cell behind the other, all flying basically the same route to the target area. The B-52 cells would fly through Laos towards the Chinese border, then southeast to Hanoi. This would take advantage of a forecast 100-knot jet stream wind blowing from northwest to southeast which would move the B-52s over the heavily defended target area quickly.

The SAC staff decided to send all available B-52s to Hanoi the first night, with slightly smaller B-52 attacks to follow on the second and third nights. The Operations staff also decided to split the attacking force into three waves, one arriving just after dark, another at midnight, and the third at four in the morning. This would, the SAC staff reasoned, keep Hanoi's citizens up all night.

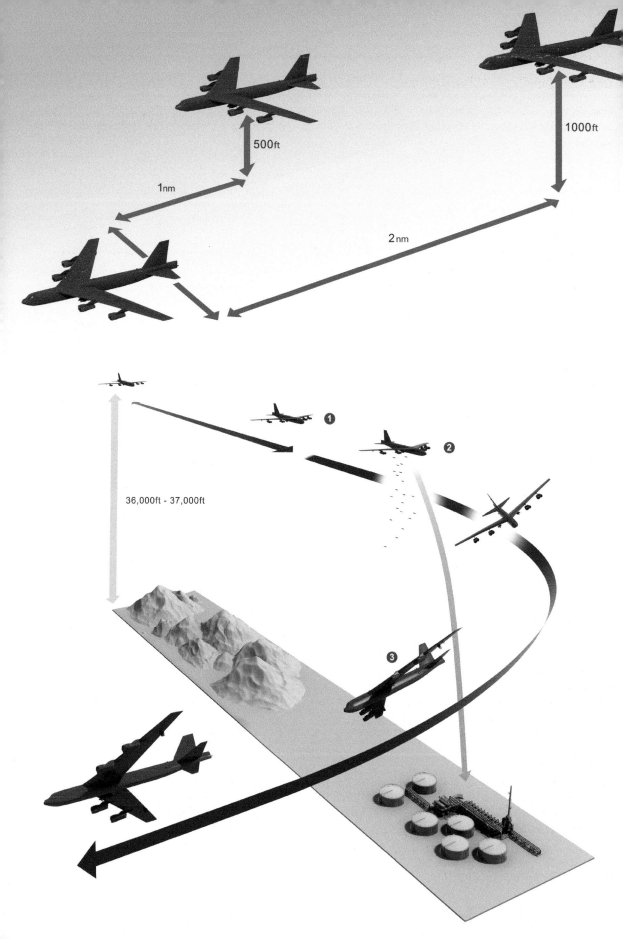

500ft

1000ft

1nm

2nm

36,000ft - 37,000ft

❶

❷

❸

OPPOSITE THE CELL FORMATION, BOMB RUN, AND THE POST-TARGET TURN

From almost the beginning of the Vietnam War B-52s flew in three-ship "cells," with the bombers one mile apart in a formation called "offset trail," and with a 500ft difference in altitude between each to avoid any risk of collisions. The cell was designed to be spread wide enough to give good bomb dispersion – the bombs were intended to hit in a rectangular "box" – while at the same time keeping the bombers close enough that they had mutual jamming support.

There were several possibilities for aiming the bombs. Usually the B-52s were guided to their targets by ground radar stations, but over North Vietnam the bombers' own bombardiers, called "radar navigators," dropped their bombs using their own radar bombsights. Additionally, the radar navigator was controlling the heading of the bomber.

Even though they were bombing the same target, each B-52 in the cell was making its own bomb run, and therefore sometimes their run-in routes were slightly different. This could diminish the bombers' mutual jamming support. For the first four nights the B-52s flew at the same altitudes they had been using for years: the lowest aircraft in the cell at 36,000ft and the highest at 37,000ft.

There was no evasive action on the bomb run. Roughly one minute from bomb release the doors were opened (**1**), time enough to go to a back-up system if the doors did not open properly. The bomb release line (**2**) was about 10 miles from the target. The post-target turn (**3**) started 30 seconds after bomb release, giving enough time to make sure that all the bombs had dropped (the B-52 had an emergency jettison if they had not) and that the bomb doors were closed.

The post-target turn was a turn to starboard at a 60-degree bank, turning at least 120 degrees from the line of the bomb run. It took about 35–50 seconds, depending on how large the turn was. However, the B-52's jammers were directional and aimed downwards, providing a zone of jamming between the aircraft and the hostile radars below. The effect of the post-target turn was to angle the jammers away to port at 60 degrees from vertical, leaving the big bomber far more visible to the North Vietnamese radars.

The post-target turn had been part of SAC high-altitude bomb delivery doctrine since the B-29s dropped the first atomic bombs, because the turn was the fastest way at high altitude to get away from a nuclear blast. It remained a standard SAC maneuver for B-52s dropping conventional bombs simply because that was how the crews had been trained. It was not until the raids on Hanoi that SAC realized the maneuver partially blanked the B-52s' jammers.

There was one other fateful decision made: because of the amount of time it took the SAC planners to draw up the mission and transmit the plan to Guam, to simplify the process the first three nights' missions would be identical – the same targets, the same times over the targets, the same entry and exit routes, and roughly the same numbers of B-52s.

Once they began to read the preliminary messages outlining the plan, the Eighth staff quickly saw the flaws. The single file of B-52s would allow the North Vietnamese to easily track one cell after the other and engage them one cell at a time. The 100-knot jet stream wind would move them through the target area quickly, but it would also give the radar navigators (bombardiers) less time to get lined up on their targets. But the major problem was that, after bomb release, the SAC plan called for the B-52s to make a steeply banked post-target turn (PTT) for 150 degrees back *into* the jet stream, a maneuver which would almost stop the bombers in mid-air over the heaviest part of the North Vietnamese SAM defenses. This seemingly innocuous post-target turn maneuver had never been tested against the captured *Fan Song* SAM radar the United States had at its test ranges, an oversight that was to have tragic consequences.

The decision to attack in three waves with four hours between each wave would minimize the risk of collisions, but it would also give North Vietnamese SAM crews a chance to engage the first wave, resupply their missile launchers before the second wave arrived, engage the second wave fully armed, then rearm their missile launchers again in time to engage the third wave.

Splitting the B-52s into three waves also diluted the support force. The reduced support force would have the greatest impact on the chaff corridor, the best countermeasure against the North Vietnamese missiles. From April to October 1972 Seventh Air Force's fighter-

bombers operating in chaff corridors had lost only one aircraft to SAMs, but there was only one squadron of 24 chaff F-4s available for the night missions. Splitting them to cover three waves meant that each B-52 wave would get only eight chaffers laying two thin corridors of chaff, one into and one out of the area, and the corridors would probably be so narrow they would not be effective. The other parts of the support force – F-4s for fighter escort to protect against MiG attack and the vital Wild Weasel F-105Gs with their much-feared anti-radiation missiles – could stay airborne for only a few hours, and three waves of B-52s with four hours between them meant that these support aircraft would also have to be split into three small groups. Overall, the result was that the support package for each wave would be *smaller* than that received by the B-52s going to much less heavily defended areas in the months before.

The Eighth Air Force staff were also very concerned about getting the planning materials from SAC in time to brief the crews, coordinate the raid with the Seventh Air Force escort support package, establish communications procedures, and a myriad of other things necessary for a large-scale raid against very heavy defenses. As the time for the first mission approached, the signs were not good. Information from SAC came in very slowly and as soon as a part of the plan arrived, SAC would follow with changes, mostly minor ones such as changes of a few minutes in times over target (TOTs), a slight change in the number of aircraft assigned to a target, or the change of a few degrees in a heading. But even minor changes had to be checked, inserted into the plan, tracking changes made, and the entire plan checked again. Additionally, there were mistakes, and every mistake had to be sent back and corrected in Omaha while the Eighth Air Force planners had to wait for the latest information to start again. To add to the problem, the communications links were becoming increasingly congested as the beginning of the operation approached, so each message was taking longer to send and each answer longer to receive. The planning process was slipping further and further behind.

The targets were also a concern. SAC forwarded a Joint Chiefs of Staff approved list of eight targets to be hit the first night – the Kinh No vehicle repair facility, the Yen Vien railroad yard, the Hanoi railroad repair shop, the Hanoi international radio station, and the MiG bases at Hoa Lac, Kep, Yen Bai, and Phuc Yen. Unfortunately, the targets selected showed a lack of understanding of the B-52s' capabilities and the North Vietnamese defenses. Some of the targets the Joint Chiefs wanted struck were small, known as "point targets," while B-52s were best suited for large "area" targets, such as storage areas and railroad yards, because the B-52s' bombing patterns spread a large number of bombs over a fairly large area. Hitting a point target was a matter of luck, even though the target area might be saturated with bombs.

A picture taken in the briefing room just before the first *Linebacker II* mission. Some remembered the first briefing as the "12 o'clock high" briefing where the curtain was drawn back exposing the route to Hanoi. (USAF)

The mission

On December 16, a stand-down was announced at all the US air bases in Southeast Asia for the next day, December 17. At Andersen, the base was filled with the sounds of engine test runs, and all day a large number of C-5 transports and KC-135 tankers took off and landed. Many of the B-52 crew members had believed Kissinger's words in late October that peace was at hand and the hopeful rumor began to spread that the B-52s were being prepared for a mass return to the US and that the C-5s were to take the maintenance personnel back. "It's over," many thought. "We're going home. The tankers are here to refuel us on our way home."

At 1400hrs on December 16 there was a briefing for all the Andersen senior commanders to give them a general outline of the mission and tell them to make sure their crews were available, but not to give any details. After the meeting, an announcement was posted that there would be a B-52 aircraft commanders' meeting the next day, December 17, at 1700hrs at the Arc Light Center.

At the briefing, the aircraft commanders were given a general overview of the missions scheduled for the next night, again told to make sure their crews were available, but cautioned not to tell their crews any specifics. The aircraft commanders left the briefing sobered, and began – frantically, in some cases – to try to locate their crews. Many of the aircraft commanders, afraid of security lapses that would warn the North Vietnamese, did not inform their crews what was coming, but many more – perhaps most – felt they had to tell their crews they would be going to Hanoi rather than going home for Christmas.

That afternoon the flight schedules were published at Andersen and for the first time the crews got an inkling of what was coming. There was a briefing for 40 crews the next morning at 1000hrs and two more large briefings at 1400hrs and 1800hrs.

The crews had a rough idea of what was to come, and many of them remember that the briefings had a "12 o'clock high" feel, up to the moment when the curtain was drawn back to show that the target was Hanoi. The crews were especially apprehensive for two reasons. Only one B-52 had been lost before, and while many of them had flown hundreds of B-52 missions they never expected the mission would be dangerous. Additionally, compared to fighter units many of the B-52 crew members were old – about 20 percent were well into their 30s – with fully developed families and much to lose.

The morning of December 17 (early in the morning of the 18th at Andersen) the Joint Chiefs sent the final attack message:

You are directed to commence at approximately 1200Z, 18 December 1972, a three-day maximum effort, repeat maximum effort, of B-52/TACAIR strikes in the Hanoi/Haiphong

A North Vietnamese propaganda picture of an SA-2 at night, but one that does hint at the difficulty of performing the loading task in the dark. (Vietnam News Agency)

area … Objective is maximum destruction of selected targets in the vicinity of Hanoi/Haiphong. Be prepared to extend beyond three days, if necessary.

Late in the afternoon of the 17th (0300hrs in Omaha) the details of the second day's (December 19/20) missions began to arrive at Eighth Air Force from SAC. The staff saw that the second day's missions had the same headings, times, and targets as the first day's missions. "We were coming in the same way the second day as we had the first day," an Eighth Air Force staff officer remembered, "like targets in a shooting gallery. I knew then our losses were going to be a lot more than 3 percent."

Night One: December 18

There were over 200 B-52s available for the operation, 53 Ds and 99 Gs from Andersen and 54 Ds from U-Tapao, and the first attack consisted of three waves of 129 B-52s. The first Hanoi wave of 48 B-52s in 16 cells had a TOT of 2000hrs Hanoi time. It was supported by 39 tactical aircraft – eight F-105G "Wild Weasels," eight F-4s laying chaff, ten F-4s for chaff escort, ten MiGCAP F-4s, and three EB-66s to the west.

The first B-52s roared off the runway at Andersen at 1451hrs local time, and at 1718hrs U-Tapao time Maple 01, the first of 21 B-52Ds, lifted off from U-Tapao. The B-52s from Guam had already been airborne for five-and-a-half hours, but the B-52s from U-Tapao would get to Hanoi first. As one crew member remembered, U-Tapao was so close that, "There was just time enough to say the Lord's Prayer, sing the Air Force Hymn and recite the 23rd Psalm and then we were on the bomb run."

The raid was a strategic surprise for the North Vietnamese but not a tactical one. When the North Vietnamese military noted the stand-down of American air activity on December 17 they realized that something was in the wind, and they also saw rescue helicopters moving close to the Thailand/Laos border. About 1000hrs two American reconnaissance drones flew over the capital and a report at 1630hrs stated that a large number of B-52s had taken off from Andersen; this was followed by reports of heavy activity at the American bases in Thailand, especially the B-52 base at U-Tapao.

The sudden, real possibility of an American attack had caught the Vietnamese on the wrong foot. A frantic order went out, canceling the leave of the 261st Regiment, which was scheduled to move south, and ordering its personnel to report back to their unit; but many of the regiment's commanders and missile crews were in remote villages with few telephones, and a mad scramble ensued to try to get the crews back.

Thirty-Six P-12 *Spoon Rest* long-range radar stations made up the first line of the North Vietnamese early warning system. At 1800hrs, 12th Company of the 290th Radar Regiment, Vietnamese People's Army Air Defense Corps, picked up jamming from EB-66s in the west and then detected the Andersen B-52s, and a few minutes later 45th Radar Company, 291st Radar Regiment, detected the U-Tapao raid. The crews knew from the jamming patterns that the returns were B-52s; they had seen B-52 radar returns many times before, but never in this number, and they watched as they moved up to a marker on their radar scopes, Point 300, the point where the B-52s normally turned west to bomb Laos or east to bomb Military Region

A model of an SA-2 launch crew in the B-52 Victory Museum, Hanoi. It shows the battalion commander on the left with his large scope, and the three controllers with their control wheels – azimuth, elevation, and altitude – on the right. (Author's collection)

Laying chaff

F-4s of the 497th Tactical Fighter Squadron, the "Nite Owls," from the 8th Tactical Fighter Wing at Ubon RTAFB laying chaff from ALE-38 chaff dispensers for the first wave of B-52s on Night One, December 18. Although chaff had been used since World War II to block radar signals, the United States did not use it in Vietnam until 1972 because it did not have a system for deploying large amounts of it. Beginning in April 1972, the Air Force began filling M-129 leaflet bombs with chaff and having Ubon-based F-4s loaded with these time-fused chaff bombs fly ahead of the B-52s in order to lay a chaff corridor for the bombers to fly through, to protect them from SAMs. The chaff corridors were not dense enough to provide complete protection, but in June 1972 the Air Force introduced the ALE-38, an external pod that could dispense chaff in a steady stream which, combined with M-129 chaff bombs, formed a dense corridor and provided excellent protection for strike flights. An F-4 "chaff bomber" usually carried four to six M-129s and one ALE-38 chaff dispenser externally, and these significantly reduced performance, so for day missions the "chaff bombers" formations were vulnerable to MiG attack and required a large fighter escort. For the night B-52 *Linebacker II* missions, the chaff-laying mission was given to a unit that specialized in night missions, Ubon's 497th Tactical Fighter Squadron, the "Nite Owls." The 497th flew the very dangerous missions attacking North Vietnamese truck convoys moving down the Ho Chi Minh trail at night, and for precise navigation at night many of the 497th F-4s were equipped with long-range navigation (LORAN) systems. When B-52s began their first missions into the heavily defended areas of North Vietnam, the 497th F-4s used LORAN for precise navigation for deploying chaff corridors for the B-52s. These early missions were nerve-wracking for the 497th crews because they were easily seen on the *Fan Song* missile radar since they were ahead of the corridor and the F-4s only had their own electronic countermeasures pods for protection; moreover the F-4s had to use their highly visible afterburners to keep at the high altitude required for the B-52 chaff corridors. Fortunately, the North Vietnamese SAMs were not fired at the chaff "bombers" but saved for the B-52s, while the few MiGs that came up also concentrated on the B-52s.

© Jim Laurier

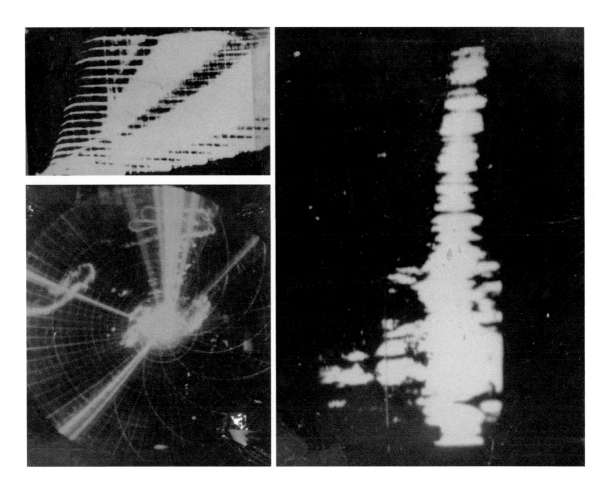

These pictures show the effects of electronic jamming and chaff on North Vietnamese radars. A non-jamming aircraft would have appeared as a single "blip" on the scope. (Author's collection)

Four. This night the B-52s moved past Point 300 following a course that US tactical aircraft used when they were attacking Hanoi. The radar company commander sent a message to his regimental headquarters that, "large numbers of B-52s appear to be on a course for Hanoi." The regiment quickly forwarded the message to the Air Defense Command headquarters in Hanoi. The streets of Hanoi were lined with public address systems and when the B-52s were about 30 miles out a "pre-alert" announcement was made. At 1850hrs the Air Defense headquarters issued a Code One alert and, as the bombers closed to within 18 miles of the city, the sirens began to wail.

The Hanoi region was the responsibility of the 361st Air Defense Division, whose heart was three SA-2 *Guideline* regiments. The 261st Regiment was responsible for the area north and east of the city, while the 257th and 274th Regiments covered the south and west. The 261st and 257th had four battalions, but the 274th was newly arrived and had only two battalions ready for combat. Because the General Staff had redeployed many of its missile battalions to the south earlier in December, there were far fewer missile units around Hanoi than there had been in 1967.

The Air Defense headquarters alerted their regiments that the B-52s were inbound, and at the battalion level the trucks that carried the missile control vans started up their engines to power their radars. As the B-52s approached, the Air Defense headquarters passed on information about the strike and assigned each regiment a target in the strike force, which the regiment passed to a battalion. The missile battalions followed the target using the battalion commander's own *Spoon Rest* search radar or the information from the headquarters. When the target came in range of the battalion's *Fan Song* guidance radar, it began to track the target and prepared to fire.

American F-111s were the first aircraft to strike, hitting MiG bases at Yen Bai, Hoa Lac, Phuc Yen, and Kep, and as the F-111s passed near Hanoi they saw that all the capital's lights were on. Off to the east and west three EB-66s were jamming the North Vietnamese radars and the eight Wild Weasel F-105Gs, as well as 20 F-4s for escort and combat air patrol (MiGCAP) over the MiG airfields, moved into position. The North Vietnamese launched a MiG-21, but it was unable to penetrate the F-4 screen.

Just before the B-52s arrived, eight F-4s began laying chaff corridors into Hanoi at 36,000ft. But the winds were almost 20 miles per hour stronger than predicted and 10 degrees off from the forecast, and the chaff corridor was blown off the B-52s' inbound course.

At 1945hrs, Snow cell and the rest of the first wave of B-52s turned towards Hanoi and their targets, the Hoa Lac airfield. As the B-52s approached Hanoi they saw it was an absolutely spectacular night, very clear with a bright, full moon over a solid white undercast at about 10,000ft, and the spectacle gave many of the American crews a surreal feeling.

Waiting for the B-52s were the North Vietnamese missile control crews in the command van of each missile battalion. Each battalion was given a target by number along with its range and bearing, and once the battalion commander received the target information he tried to locate the target with his *Spoon Rest* search radar. As the B-52s approached, the only noise in the van besides the voices of the crews was that of loud cooling fans, necessary to cool the vacuum tubes of the relatively primitive electronics of the SA-2 system.

As the B-52s approached, the jamming from the bombers and their escorts began to appear on the missile battalions' radarscopes. The official North Vietnamese history of the operation described these first minutes:

> The atmosphere in the command headquarters at every level was extremely strained at this time. We did not have much experience and were not effective. Almost all the missile units responsible for protecting Hanoi had never seen a B-52 signal on their screen. Though they had been trained early on paper, it was only in theory. In battle, there is a very wide gap between theory and practice. The B-52s' signals were drowned in a jumbled mass of fake signals from the B-52s themselves, the signals of the escort planes, as well as the signals of EB-66 planes flying outside the formation and other decoy signals. F-4s were spreading decoy signals over a wide corridor. These operations caused us many difficulties in discovering and striking the enemy. All the radar returns were buried in a jamming curtain of bright, white fog. The screen of the guidance officer and the tracking operators showed many dark green stripes slanted together, changing at abnormal speeds, one strobe overriding and mixing with another, this stripe joining that one and splitting away. After that, hundreds and thousands of bright dots specked the screens like bunches of target blips moving sluggishly. With all that mass confusion coupled with a constant blinking like a downpour of rain, how were we expected to distinguish between [fighter] type jamming and [bomber] type jamming, or which was EB-66 jamming, and which was the passive type metallic chaff strewn across the sky by F-4s?

The first missile sites the B-52s met as they moved down from the northwest were the missile battalions of the 261st Missile Regiment. Tension mounted as the missile crews continued trying to track the B-52s passively on their *Spoon Rest* search radar by following the jamming strobes instead of using their *Fan Song* radars in the active mode and risking an attack by anti-radiation missiles, but the jamming was too intense. The 78th Battalion commander took a risk and turned on his *Fan Song* tracking radar to try to pick up the B-52s, and a few seconds later broke out a single B-52 jamming strobe on his *Fan Song* radar scope. The battalion commander put the cross hairs on the strobe and the radar return appeared on the scopes of the three officers who were responsible for tracking the target and controlling the missiles' course in range, azimuth, and elevation.

Gia Lam International Airport was "off limits" because it was an international airfield, but a frustrated B-52 crew deliberately targeted it. Ironically, after *Linebacker II* was over this picture was used by the Chairman of the Joint Chiefs of Staff to show Congress how accurate and effective the B-52 bombing was. (Author's collection)

When there was no jamming the radar could be set to automatically track the target, but when the target was jamming the return was too unstable and the missile had to be guided manually; the crew turned their steering wheels to keep the strobe centered in their scopes so that the missile could follow the radar beam to the target. At 1945hrs, the commander pushed one fire button and then, six seconds later, the second, after which he reported the firing to the regimental headquarters. The missiles missed, but there was a sigh of relief at the Air Defense headquarters – now they knew they would be giving the B-52s a battle, and soon the remaining battalions opened fire.

Seven miles above the city, the B-52s' electronic warfare officers were involved in a silent battle using their multiple manually operated jammers. The skill of the electronic warfare officer was vital, and one later described the situation:

> They make a move and you counter. They change frequency and you adjust your jammer to the new frequency. The SAM operators used every trick they knew – shifting frequency, acquiring from one site and shooting from another and various other tricks. We relied on mutual support jamming from other aircraft in the cell and it was probably our best defense in hindsight. I would see several uplink signals on my ALR-20 receiver simultaneously during

the bomb run, which indicated SAM ... I distinctly remember the jamming signals were so heavy on my receiver, that it was difficult to see my own jamming. We were told to jam the downlink frequency (that the missile used to communicate with the ground site) whenever we saw an uplink signal. The ALT-28 was our primary transmitter against the *Fan Song* radar and we used a track-while-scan [TS] mode that created multiple strobes that walked off the tracking gate and caused them to try to reacquire a target ...

During the post-target turn, we were in a 60-degree right bank, which pointed the lobes from the left side toward the sky and very possibly the right wing interfered with the radiation lobes on the right side. However, in my decidedly non-engineering opinion, burn-through from the close proximity of the SAM sites was more important and we also turned into a 100-knot headwind that significantly slowed us down during egress.

As the North Vietnamese began to fire their missiles, the American crews were treated to a spectacular, if deadly, show. When the SAM booster rockets fired, the flare of the huge motors was diffused and magnified under the clouds, and one of the pilots described the scene:

An area about the size of a city block was lit up by the flash and it looked as if the whole city block had caught fire ... As the missile broke through the clouds, the diffused large lighted area was replaced by a ring of silver fire that appeared to be the size of a basketball. This was the exhaust of rocket motor that would grow brighter as the missile approached the aircraft ... from the front quarter, it took on the appearance of a lighted silver doughnut.

Another B-52 aircraft commander remembered:

It's really easy to describe it as a telephone pole with a 15ft stream of flame behind it. You don't actually see the missile until it's very, very, very close and then you can see the outline, if there's any moon at all. And the biggest thing you see is the tail of the thing. And of course, the next biggest thing you see is when it detonates a nice big elliptical ring of fire that's shooting steel ball bearings out at you. Actually, it's real pretty if it doesn't kill you.

When the missiles missed and their rocket motors ran out of fuel, the missile warheads exploded; they became huge fireballs sending out ribbons of luminescent fragments.

The first B-52 shoot-down

A missile site of the 93rd Battalion, 261st Regiment firing its SA-2s at the first wave of B-52s, Night One. The first B-52 to be shot down, Charcoal 01, has just been hit. This first night the North Vietnamese missile battalions possessed a full load of missiles, and had all six of their launchers with missiles mounted, as well as six ZIL trucks, each with a new missile, waiting in a holding area to come to the launcher as soon as the missile was fired. With this number of missiles, the missile crews were able to follow Soviet missile doctrine and fire three missiles at every target, guided by the *Fan Song* radar on the far right side of the picture. The closest missile is taking off using its booster rocket, which will fire for 4–5 seconds and then drop off. The missiles in flight in the background are using their main sustainer engine which will fire for 22 seconds. The empty launcher in the foreground has fired its missile and has dropped into the horizontal position so that the missile crew can load a new missile from the ZIL truck pulling up in front of the empty launcher. Once the truck's missile was unloaded, it proceeded to an area away from the site where new missiles were waiting. Prior to *Linebacker II* the Americans had only sent in one tactical strike flight a day, so the sites had possessed enough missiles to engage all the flights. The problem that occurred quickly during *Linebacker II* – in fact, by the second night – was that many more missiles were fired, and so there was a shortage of assembled missiles. The SA-2 took the missile regiment's technical battalion several hours to assemble and fuel, and only two of the three missile regiments had a technical battalion available, so the assembly process was further delayed. When there was a break in the attacks on December 25 to December 26, more missiles were assembled in Hanoi and additional missiles brought from Haiphong, but the massive attacks on December 26 and December 27 practically exhausted the North Vietnamese missile supply.

The first B-52 shot down over Hanoi was Charcoal 01 and the radar navigator, Major Fernando Alexander, was "introduced" to the international press. (Vietnam News Agency)

The first seven cells, all from U-Tapao, had dropped their bombs, come through unscathed and turned towards home as the next group of 33 B-52s moved in to attack the huge storage area at Kinh No, just north of Hanoi.

Lilac was the second cell and Lilac 03 was hit by a SAM 30 seconds prior to bomb release. The SAM exploded on the left side of the aircraft, puncturing most of the fuel tanks, knocking out the instruments and electrical power and damaging its bomb release system so none of the bombs released. The aircraft commander was hit in the left eye and almost blinded by shrapnel, so the copilot took over the aircraft and flew it to U-Tapao where it landed safely, the first victim of the SA-2s during the operation.

The next casualty came from Charcoal cell, one of three B-52G cells attacking the Yen Vien railroad. Charcoal 01 was one of the "unmodified" G models with the lower powered ALT-6B jammers, and the North Vietnamese SAM operators apparently overpowered the system.

The North Vietnamese Air Defense Command headquarters passed the Charcoal cell to 59th Battalion, which fired two missiles using "three-point" guidance, and they executed the difficult control maneuver well. One missile hit Charcoal 01 in the forward section and started a fire in the front wheel well, then nosed down as the crew ejected. An F-4 escort noted: "The first B-52 in the cell was hit and we watched in amazement as the giant airplane cracked open like an egg, followed by a surrealistic scene of raining fire as it slowly fell toward the ground burning almost all the way." Three of the crew were captured and three died.

The 59th had an observer in the optical guidance cabinet on the missile control van and he began to shout: "It's burning! It's a big fire! There is one big cloud of smoke like the one in the atomic bomb explosion in the north." The 59th reported its kill, and the North

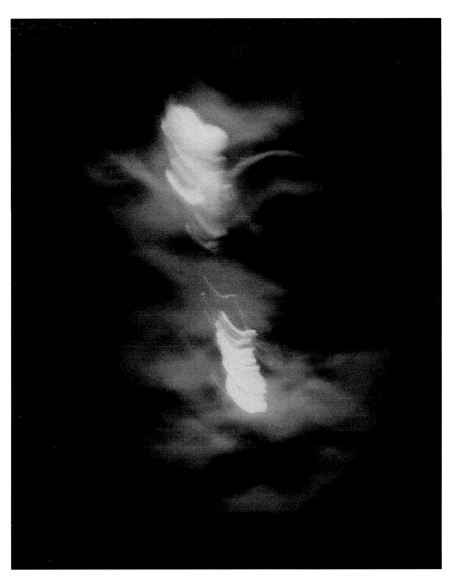

On Night One, Charcoal 01 became the first B-52 to be lost to an SA-2 during *Linebacker II*. (Vietnam News Agency)

Vietnamese Air Defense headquarters exploded with joy, the members of the Air Defense staff embracing each other.

As the first wave of B-52s withdrew, the North Vietnamese missile battalions regrouped. The battalion commanders sent their missile trucks to the storage warehouses to replace the missiles they had fired with new ones. It was a time-consuming process as the trucks picked their way through the narrow streets and burning buildings, having to stop from time to time and turn back to find another route when one was blocked by debris.

Four hours later the second American raid, an all-Andersen group of 18 B-52Gs and 12 B-52Ds, arrived. The support package was basically the same as for the first wave, and once again, just before the B-52s arrived, eight F-4s began laying chaff corridors into Hanoi at 36,000ft. But the winds remained stronger than the forecast and were still 10 degrees off, and once again the chaff corridor was blown off the B-52s' inbound course.

Peach cell, a mixture of modified and unmodified B-52Gs, was the first cell over the rail yards at Yen Vien. Peach 02 had just released its bombs and begun its post-target turn when a SAM hit set the two outboard engines on fire. Peach 02 headed for Thailand and made it across the border, but fire forced the crew to bail out and they had barely cleared the aircraft when the B-52 dissolved in a huge explosion. Within 20 minutes rescue helicopters picked up all the crew members.

On this second wave, there was a real breakdown of discipline. The Gia Lam International Airport was off limits to bombing because it was used by civilian flights, but such niceties were of no concern to one frustrated crew flying a Guam B-52D. Gia Lam was an easily identified target for the radar bombardier, and the big bomber drifted slightly, almost imperceptibly, off the west of the bomb run heading, and unloaded its bombs on the airport. The bombing was spectacularly accurate, cratering several runways and destroying about 80 percent of the international terminal.

To the south of Hanoi, the 77th Battalion of the 257th Regiment had made what would turn out to be a breakthrough in its efforts against the American bombers. The commander saw that after the B-52s dropped their bombs their jamming dropped off and at that point a B-52 could be tracked automatically. In fact, the 77th Battalion had found a major vulnerability in the B-52s' tactics.

At a little before 0400hrs the third wave of 30 B-52s arrived. This wave had 40 support aircraft but no Air Force Wild Weasels; instead, it had four Navy A-7E Weasels as well as additional Navy jamming aircraft, five EA-3Bs plus three Air Force EB-66s. As before, eight F-4s began laying chaff corridors into Hanoi but the winds remained different than predicted and again the chaff corridor was blown off the B-52s' inbound course.

The 77th Battalion watched the raid come in and was assigned to attack Rose cell. The 77th launched two missiles into the jamming strobe with three-point guidance but when Rose 01 rolled into its post-target turn the jet stream wind slowed it down dramatically and, as the missile battalion commander expected, suddenly the return appeared very clearly. The missile crew changed to the autotrack mode, and Rose 01 was hit and crashed in the Hanoi suburbs.

As the B-52s retired, the North Vietnamese air defense units all over the country inundated the Air Defense headquarters with messages asking one question: "Is it true you have shot down B-52s over Hanoi?" When the headquarters confirmed the kills, the staff and the victorious missile battalions were overwhelmed by congratulations. The North Vietnamese leaders were not the only ones to appreciate what happened that night. As the sun rose, curious Hanoi citizens flocked to the wreckage of the two B-52s which crashed close to the missile sites that had brought them down. Major Fernando Alexander, the radar navigator from Rose 01, was "introduced" to the foreign press at the Hanoi International Club.

For the expenditure of fewer than 130 SA-2s, the missile crews had brought down three B-52s and badly damaged two. The Chief of Air Defense Staff were satisfied but realized that the Americans would be coming during the day with their deadly laser-guided bombs. He therefore divided the air defense system, with the SAM battalions taking major responsibility for the expected nightly B-52 raids while the daytime missions were left to the MiGs, which had been very effective during the *Linebacker I* day attacks.

Meanwhile, there was a slowly developing crisis with the supply of SA-2 missiles. Each battalion had begun the first night with 12 missiles: six on their launchers and six more on trucks that moved in and reloaded the launchers after the missiles were fired. But there were very few missiles pre-assembled in the three nearby storage warehouses, two of which were in Hanoi and one on the other side of the Red River. After the first night's battles many of the battalions were short of missiles. By morning there were long lines of trucks outside the technical units' warehouses waiting for new missiles, and reports had already come in of problems during the seemingly interminable waits at the missile warehouses.

In the storage area each regiment had a technical battalion which was responsible for the assembly of the SA-2 missiles and the maintenance of the launcher. The 257th and

After the first "invincible" B-52 was shot down, crowds of Hanoi residents flocked to the wreckage. The wreckage of every B-52 shot down in the city was left for the people to see. (Vietnam News Agency)

After the failure to shoot down any B-52s on Night Two, all the missile battalion commanders were called to headquarters to explain their failure, then told to go out and tell their crews to do better on Night Three. (Vietnam News Agency)

261st Regiments each had a technical battalion on site, but the 274th Regiment's technical battalion had still not arrived from the south so it had to depend on the other regiments to supply them with missiles.

On the US side, of the five B-52s hit, three were hit just prior to reaching the target and the other two B-52s in the post-target turn, the two occasions at which experienced crew members believed the B-52s were most vulnerable. The missile battalions were all near to the targets, and when the B-52s were close to the *Fan Song* it was easier for the radar to overpower – "burn through" – the jamming. When B-52s opened their bomb bay doors it increased their radar signature tremendously, making the *Fan Song's* radar task much easier. After that, exactly when the bomb bay doors closed, the bombers went into their steeply banked post-target turn and blanked their jamming antennas. This turn was made even worse by the fact that it was made into the jet stream winds, which slowed the bombers' ground speed by 100 knots, almost stopping them in mid-air and holding them suspended over the heavily defended target area. Many of the crews believed that this was the reason the two bombers were hit at this time.

Another cause for concern was that two of the three aircraft lost had been G models – two-thirds of the first night's losses, even though they were only about one quarter of the overall force. Although SAC had told Eighth Air Force that the unmodified Gs were just as effective as the modified Gs, the Eighth had already expressed doubts about the tests and were watching the unmodified G models carefully.

There were two other major problems for the escort force. Because of the three waves, the chaffers had been divided into three groups that were really too small to lay anything other than a thin corridor, which had been quickly blown away by the unforecast winds. Another major problem was that the mission plan had arrived late to the Wild Weasel squadrons, and even when it did so it had not included the B-52s' entry and exit headings; this meant that the Wild Weasels could not parallel the bombers and be pointed at the SAM sites in order to be in a position to launch their anti-radiation missiles as soon as the *Fan Song* radar came on.

Back in the United States, Nixon and his staff expected outrage, but for whatever reason – the winter weather, the approach of the Christmas holidays, satisfaction that the United States was finally doing something, or simple war-weariness – there were no massive demonstrations.

While missions were in the air, the Eighth Air Force staff had received the mission plans for Night Three from SAC. They were virtually the same as for Night One and Night Two – the same times, routes, altitudes, and targets.

Night Two: December 19

On Night Two, 93 B-52 missions were scheduled against Hanoi. The first raid would be entirely from Andersen, with nine Gs and 12 Ds, and the target for most of this raid was the Kinh No complex, which had been bombed by each of the three raids the night before. There were no changes in the mission patterns from the night before, other than a variation of a few thousand feet in altitude and different spacing between the cells, nothing the North Vietnamese would even notice. The support package was roughly the same as the first night, but with fewer MiGCAP fighters.

At the end of the briefing for the first raid, the Andersen wing commander, Colonel James McCarthy, stunned the crews when he announced that any aircraft commander who maneuvered to evade SAMs prior to bomb release would be court-martialed. Then, when the first raid was heading for its targets, the crews of the second raid – 21 Gs from Andersen and 15 Ds from U-Tapao – began their briefing by being told that evasive maneuvering was now approved so long as the bombers were straight and level at bomb release. It was almost surreal – the crews of the first wave had gone to Hanoi under Colonel McCarthy's threat of court-martial if they maneuvered, while the second-wave crews four hours later were actually encouraged to maneuver.

At U-Tapao the short missions meant that their crews could fly every day, and the second night's missions included many of the crews that had flown the first night. After the first night's losses, it was chilling for these crews to see that the whole force was coming in on the same headings, at the same altitudes, bombing the same targets and using the same post-target turn in an area where the crews noted that the SAMs seemed to be heaviest.

In Hanoi, the Air Defense headquarters told the missile crews to expect the B-52s to follow the same route and bomb the same targets as the night before, and they were all confident that they were going to inflict severe losses on the B-52s.

But perhaps because the headquarters of the 361st Missile Division was moving to a different location to avoid an American air attack, the North Vietnamese air defenses faltered badly on Night Two. In the 12-minute first-wave raid all the SAMs missed – not a single B-52 was even damaged despite the narrow chaff corridor again being blown away by high winds.

The second raid arrived over Hanoi four hours later and was less well supported, with only two F-4 chaffers. Nine B-52Gs bombed Hanoi Radio, in the heart of the SAM batteries, but once again the SAM crews faltered; and only one G model was slightly damaged. Six U-Tapao Ds that arrived later received a different reception. Ivory 01 dropped its bombs but was hit by a SA-2 in its post-target turn and with one engine on fire, cables for the rudder and right elevator severed and both drop tanks holed, it headed for the nearest emergency base in Thailand where it crash landed.

Right on schedule, four hours after the second raid the third raid arrived, six Gs and 15 Ds from Andersen and 15 Ds from U-Tapao. The support package was stronger, with

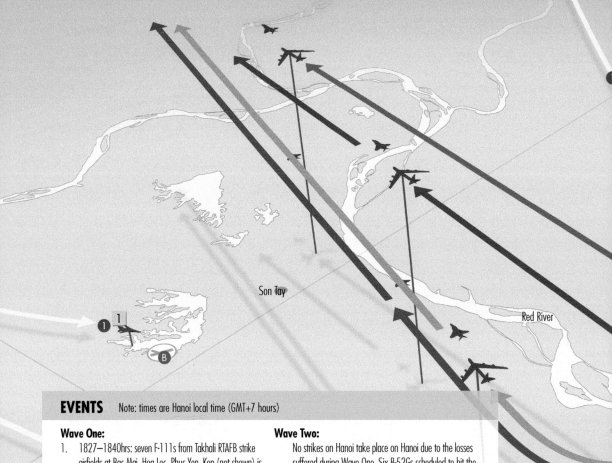

Son Tay

Red River

B

EVENTS   Note: times are Hanoi local time (GMT+7 hours)

Wave One:

1. 1827–1840hrs: seven F-111s from Takhali RTAFB strike airfields at Bac Mai, Hoa Loc, Phuc Yen. Kep (not shown) is also attacked at this time.

2. 1840hrs: eight F-4s from 8th TFW based at Ubon begin to drop chaff, accompanied by five 8th TFW F-4 escorts.

3. 1850hrs: 10 F-4 MiG CAP (not shown) and 10 F-4 B-52 escorts from the 432nd TRW based at Udorn are on station.

4. 1850hrs: four F-4Cs Wild Weasels, four F-105G Wild Weasels, and three EB-66E from the 388th TFW (not shown) based at Korat are on station.

5. 2000hrs: two cells of six B-52Ds (Snow and Lilac) from Andersen attack the Hanoi Railroad Complex.

6. 2009hrs: four cells of 12 B-52Gs (Quilt, Gold, Wine, Brass) from Andersen attack Yen Vien, north of the Duong River.

7. 2009hrs: Quilt 03 (a B-52G) is shot down 5 miles north of Hanoi by the 93rd Missile Battalion.

8. 2020hrs: Brass 02 (a B-52G) is hit by a SAM from the 94th Missile Battalion. It will crash during egress in Thailand.

9. 2026hrs: five cells of 15 B-52Ds (Snow, Grape, Orange, Black, Ebony) from U-Tapao attack Yen Vien.

10. 2032hrs: Orange 03 (a B-52D) is shot down by the 94th Missile Battalion just north of Hanoi.

Wave Two:

No strikes on Hanoi take place on Hanoi due to the losses suffered during Wave One. Six B-52Gs scheduled to hit the Hanoi railroad repair shops are recalled.

Wave Three:

11. 0440hrs: eight F-4 chaff bombers and five F-4 escorts from the 8th TFW begin to lay a chaff corridor.

12. 0440hrs: ten F-4s flying MiG CAP from the 432nd TRW and three EB-66Es from the 388th TFW at Korat arrive on station, joined by four Navy A-6As for SAM suppression and five EA-3Bs for jamming support (not shown).

13. 0508hrs: ten F-4s escorting the B-52s arrive on station.

14. 0508hrs: three cells of nine B-52Ds (Chestnut, Bleach, Straw) from Andersen AFB attack the Hanoi railroad repair shops.

15. 0511hrs: Straw 02 is hit by a SAM from the 93rd Missile Battalion. It will crash during egress in northern Laos.

16. 0512hrs: four cells of 12 B-52Gs (Olive, Ruby, Tan, Aqua) from Andersen attack the Kien No complex.

17. 0512hrs: Olive 1 (a B-52G) is shot down by the 57th Missile Battalion. It crashes 9 miles north of Hanoi.

18. 0515hrs: Tan 03 (a B-52G) is shot down by the 57th Missile Battalion. It crashes in Hanoi.

19. 0528–0539hrs: four cells of 12 B-52Ds (Walnut, Red, Lime, Brick) from U-Tapao bomb the Hanoi petroleum product storage area without loss. Brick 02 is slightly damaged by a SAM but is recovered at U-Tapao.

Night Three

December 20, 1972

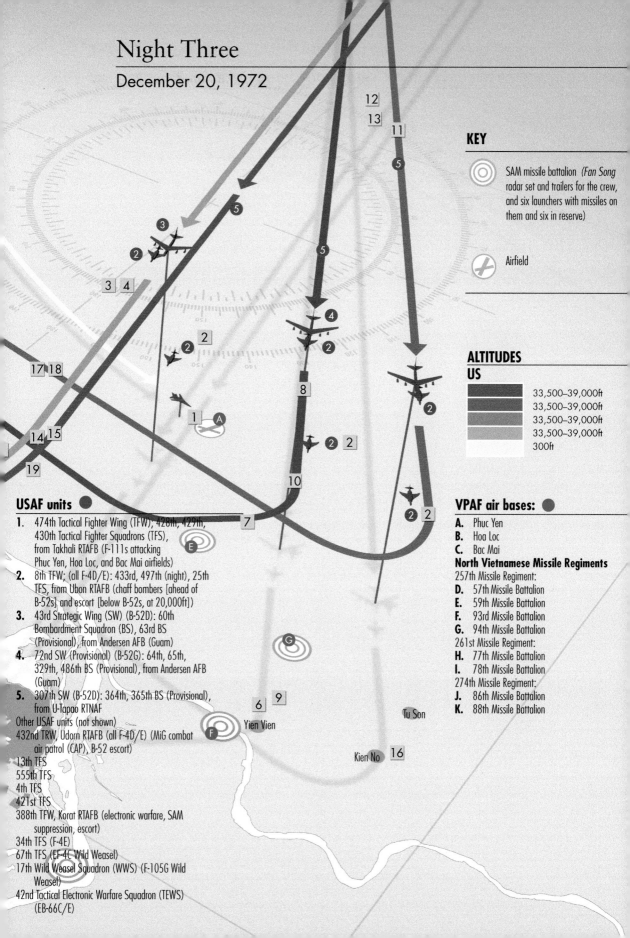

KEY

◎ SAM missile battalion *(Fan Song* radar set and trailers for the crew, and six launchers with missiles on them and six in reserve)

✈ Airfield

ALTITUDES

US

▬	33,500–39,000ft
▬	33,500–39,000ft
▬	33,500–39,000ft
▬	33,500–39,000ft
▬	300ft

VPAF air bases: ●

A. Phuc Yen
B. Hoa Loc
C. Bac Mai

North Vietnamese Missile Regiments

257th Missile Regiment:
D. 57th Missile Battalion
E. 59th Missile Battalion
F. 93rd Missile Battalion
G. 94th Missile Battalion

261st Missile Regiment:
H. 77th Missile Battalion
I. 78th Missile Battalion

274th Missile Regiment:
J. 86th Missile Battalion
K. 88th Missile Battalion

USAF units ●

1. 474th Tactical Fighter Wing (TFW), 428th, 429th, 430th Tactical Fighter Squadrons (TFS), from Takhali RTAFB (F-111s attacking Phuc Yen, Hoa Loc, and Bac Mai airfields)
2. 8th TFW; (all F-4D/E): 433rd, 497th (night), 25th TFS, from Ubon RTAFB (chaff bombers [ahead of B-52s] and escort [below B-52s, at 20,000ft])
3. 43rd Strategic Wing (SW) (B-52D): 60th Bombardment Squadron (BS), 63rd BS (Provisional), from Andersen AFB (Guam)
4. 72nd SW (Provisional) (B-52G): 64th, 65th, 329th, 486th BS (Provisional), from Andersen AFB (Guam)
5. 307th SW (B-52D): 364th, 365th BS (Provisional), from U-Tapao RTNAF

Other USAF units (not shown)
432nd TRW, Udorn RTAFB (all F-4D/E) (MiG combat air patrol (CAP), B-52 escort)
13th TFS
555th TFS
4th TFS
421st TFS
388th TFW, Korat RTAFB (electronic warfare, SAM suppression, escort)
34th TFS (F-4E)
67th TFS (EF-4C Wild Weasel)
17th Wild Weasel Squadron (WWS) (F-105G Wild Weasel)
42nd Tactical Electronic Warfare Squadron (TEWS) (EB-66C/E)

Yien Vien

Tu Son

Kien No

eight chaffers and Navy jamming aircraft, and again the B-52s were revisiting targets, one of them the Yen Vien complex. But the nine B-52Ds that struck Yen Vien found the North Vietnamese response anemic – only ten SAMs were counted, and no B-52s were hit. The other 27 B-52s bombed a safe target far from Hanoi, the Thai Nguyen thermal power plant, with little North Vietnamese reaction and no damage.

The North Vietnamese Air Defense Command staff were devastated by the failure to shoot down any B-52s on Night Two when the B-52s had repeated the pattern of Night One. They realized that the movement of the division headquarters was partially responsible since the division could not provide leadership or coordinate the attacks and the crews were still inexperienced with the B-52s; but a more serious problem was that fewer missiles were delivered than had been fired the first night, and the crews were already afraid of running out of missiles. As the stocks dwindled, a phenomenon that the missile crews called "missile fever," the fear of running out of missiles, was already beginning to emerge.

Despite having been in battle all night, all the Hanoi area missile battalion commanders were called to the Air Defense headquarters to critique what went wrong. One by one, the exhausted and humiliated battalion commanders had to stand in front of their counterparts and the staff and explain the techniques they had used, why they failed, and what they planned on doing to improve their results. The headquarters staff listened, then gave the commanders a simple message – they would have to find a way to defeat the enemy. There could be no excuses about missile shortage, jamming or anything else. They had a chance to fight their own great, decisive battle, an "aerial Dien Bien Phu," and they had to be smart enough to overcome the Americans' technology. The commanders were then sent back for a few hours' sleep, knowing they would have another battle that night.

The Air Defense Command leaders saw that the B-52s had used the northwest–southeast route to Hanoi the two previous nights, and the leaders decided that the US would repeat the same routes and tactics. Two SAM battalions moved from the south to the north of the city and deployed so that their missile sites would form a triangle around Hanoi with the point to the northwest, which would allow the sites to fire at the B-52s coming down from the northwest much further out.

The headquarters' SA-2 experts also realized that techniques that took advantage of the B-52s' standardized tactics appeared to offer the best chance of success. The B-52s' altitudes and maneuver were known and at certain points the B-52s' jamming decreased, though the North Vietnamese did not know exactly why. The experts recommended firing the missiles initially with manual guidance at the jamming strobe, then transferring the missile guidance to automatic tracking while the missile was in the air when the bomber's radar return became clear. The technical officers also realized that the closer a B-52 was to the missile site, the better were the chances of going to automatic tracking, so they told the battalion commanders to delay their firings and wait for close range, to go "face to face with the B-52s."

While the North Vietnamese were making adjustments in light of their experience from the previous two nights, the American forces were not. The SAC leadership was especially satisfied that no B-52s had been shot down and felt that their planning, tactics, and the concept of planning at headquarters rather than in the field were validated. But while SAC was satisfied with the results of the first two days, the staffs and crews in the combat zone were not. Even though no B-52s had been lost on the second night many of the crews had received a heavy dose of SAMs and they saw little slackening in the North Vietnamese defenses. At U-Tapao, General Glenn Sullivan had been working hard with the crews trying to find out what the problems were with the tactics and had been forwarding suggestions to Eighth Air Force and on to SAC, where they seemed to disappear.

At Andersen, where the G wing had lost two aircraft the first night, there remained considerable apprehension about their electronic countermeasures suite, as well as a certain amount of frustration that the Gs were forced to go to Hanoi with only 27 bombs. This frustration was exacerbated by the regular failures of the Gs' release system – during the first two nights five Gs had had some sort of a bomb release problem.

Night Three: December 20

When the crews from U-Tapao and Andersen went in for their briefings for the third night's missions and saw that they would be flying the same routes to the same targets for the third night in a row, according to one of the briefers the news produced "emotions from serious concern to outright disgust."

The first wave of the third night consisted of 33 B-52s in 11 cells, with nine of these cells targeted on Yen Vien, which had been bombed on both the first and second nights. Quilt cell, consisting of G models, led nine cells from Andersen, and inbound two of the Gs, Quilt 01 and Quilt 03, each lost two jammers.

The North Vietnamese defenders watched on their radar scopes as a narrow chaff corridor unfolded and again the high winds blew it through the area rapidly. The corridor showed that the B-52s were heading for Hanoi again, and at the Air Defense headquarters, General Tran smiled with satisfaction when he saw "an extraordinary thing ... the enemy continued to concentrate his attacks on Hanoi ....using the same old tricks and jamming techniques."

All the Hanoi missile battalions watched the raid approach and waited anxiously for orders to engage, but none more anxiously than the members of the 93rd Missile Battalion, who had been harshly criticized that afternoon for their tracking techniques. As 93rd Battalion watched the B-52s, they were both pleased and amazed: "the extraordinary thing was that tonight the [B-52s] followed exactly the same flight path [as the previous nights]. They never thought that in one day their adversaries could change their tactics."

As the B-52s approached, the headquarters called and told the 93rd to engage the third cell of B-52s, Quilt cell, which had two unmodified Gs, 01 and 03. The 93rd fired two missiles at long range, but both missed. At 12 miles the 93rd fired two more missiles and then, while their missiles were in flight, Quilt 03 made its post-target turn. Quilt 03 had lost two jammers inbound and the missile battalion commander easily broke out the B-52, went to automatic tracking and shot down Quilt 03.

The news that the 93rd had shot down a B-52 both exhilarated and relaxed the headquarters staff because they knew the lessons had taken hold. More good results quickly followed.

Brass cell, another cell of G models, followed Quilt. The formation was spread out and Brass 02 had three jammers out, and that was all the 94th Missile Battalion needed to burn

Tan 03 is hit over Kinh No

On Night Three, December 20, the B-52G models in the first wave of three planned waves had suffered such heavy losses that the G models in the second raid had been called back – the first time an American strategic bombing raid had ever been turned back by defenses. However, despite the first wave losses, SAC decided to have the B-52Gs in the third wave continue to attack targets in Hanoi. In this third wave Tan, a cell of three B-52Gs, was attacking the Kinh No storage complex 9 miles north of Hanoi, a target that had been bombed every night. Kinh No was one of the most dangerous *Linebacker II* targets during the raids – four B-52s were hit by SA-2s bombing Kinh No and three shot down. When the third wave attacked, a B-52 was quickly shot down from Olive cell, the cell in front of Tan which was also bombing Kinh No. The first two B-52Gs in Tan cell had the most powerful jamming equipment while Tan 03 had older, lower-powered jammers, and Tan 03 also had two jammers out and bombing systems problems. While trying to line up on the bomb run, Tan 03 moved away from the other two B-52s in the cell and lost their jamming support. At this point in the attack the North Vietnamese were very short of missiles and the 57th Missile Battalion of the 261st Missile Regiment had only one missile left, but Tan 03's position and its lack of jamming power allowed the 57th's commander to break out a single jamming strobe and launch this last missile in full autotrack. Tan 03 was 12 miles from Kinh No and was just preparing to drop its bombs when the 57th's missile struck the forward fuselage and Tan 03 disintegrated. The gunner, Staff Sergeant James L. Lollar, bailed out just after the explosion and was the only survivor.

through when Brass 02 went into its post-target turn. The battalion launched two missiles in rapid succession using automatic tracking. Brass 02 was hit but was able to stagger across the border to Thailand where the crew bailed out.

Five cells of B-52Ds from U-Tapao began their attack on Yen Vien and the 77th Battalion fired two missiles at Orange cell, the third of the five cells, and broke out Orange 03 as the cell opened its bomb doors and the radar return mushroomed. The missiles arrived just before Orange 03 released its bombs, hitting it squarely in the bomb bay. There was a tremendous explosion that was seen by an American RC-135 orbiting more than 80 miles away over the Gulf of Tonkin, but, amazingly, two of the crew of Orange 03 survived.

As each of the B-52s was going down, a female voice announced the kill over a loudspeaker at the Air Defense Command Center, but then came the voice of the duty officer of the technical section – the 77th Battalion was out of missiles. This announcement was immediately followed by the report that the 94th Battalion was also out of missiles.

At Seventh Air Force in Saigon there was profound shock over the three B-52s lost in the first raid and they quickly contacted Eighth Air Force, who immediately called SAC and told them the situation – almost 10 percent of the first raid had been shot down, including two of 12 G models; now the second raid of 27 B-52s, including six G models, was on its way to North Vietnam to attack the Hanoi railroad yard in the heart of the Hanoi defenses. General Meyer accordingly made the decision to call the six Gs targeted for Hanoi back to Andersen.

Thus, the North Vietnamese defenses had done something that the Germans, Japanese, Russians, Chinese, and North Koreans had never been able to achieve – they had made the Americans abort a bombing raid for fear of losses. Ironically, if the second wave had continued, the Gs would have met mainly empty missile launchers. For the first time, an opportunity was missed for the United States to find out that the North Vietnamese were out of missiles. It would not be the last.

After General Meyer's order to cancel the second raid of G models, the question still remained as to what to do with the Gs in the third raid, which had four cells of G models, a total of 12 aircraft. They would be dropping only 324 bombs, fewer than a single cell of B-52Ds, and all were scheduled to hit the Kinh No complex just a few miles north of Hanoi, so that the Gs' post-target turns would take place over the heaviest concentration of North Vietnamese SA-2 sites. A postwar official Air Force history noted: "It was apparent [after the first raid losses] that the unmodified Gs were neither protecting themselves nor the formations adequately and were bearing the brunt of the losses inflicted by Hanoi's SAM sites." It was clear that sending the Gs on the third raid to Hanoi was close to a suicide mission.

But the SAC staff were clearly disturbed that General Meyer had canceled the second raid. General Harry Cordes, SAC's Chief of Intelligence, said, "[We] wanted to prove that SAC could do the job," so the order was given for the B-52Gs to continue.

On the ground, two battalions were still out of missiles, but the rest of the missile battalions had been at least partially resupplied as the North Vietnamese watched the third raid move down towards Hanoi.

Straw 02, a B-52D in one of the cells ahead of the Guam Gs, was 10 miles from the chaff corridor in its post-target turn when it was hit by a missile from the 78th Battalion of the 257th Regiment. Straw 02 made it to Laos where the crew bailed out. One minute after Straw 02 was hit, Olive, a G model cell, began its bomb run on Kinh No, but the cell had lost its integrity and had no mutual ECM coverage. Olive 01 was hit and went down like a torch about 9 miles north of Hanoi, and only two of the six crew members survived. This was the third kill for the 77th Battalion, but – fortunately for the Americans – the site had been only partially resupplied and had used its last missiles to down Olive 01.

Tan cell followed and also lost cell integrity and mutual jamming support. On the ground below, the 57th Missile Battalion had only one missile left but its radar operators were able to break out a single jamming strobe and launched the missile in full autotrack as the B-52 approached to 12 miles. Tan 03, an unmodified G, was still far from the rest of Tan cell when the 57th's missile stuck the forward fuselage. The gunner bailed out just before Tan 03 disintegrated.

Just after the loss of Tan 03, four cells of B-52Ds attacked the Hanoi petroleum storage area, but the North Vietnamese sites had only a few missiles left; Brick 02 was hit but only slightly damaged.

As the last B-52s departed, the North Vietnamese were ecstatic. In less than ten minutes, they had shot down three B-52s using only 35 missiles, and overall four of the giant bombers had crashed in the Hanoi suburbs. Their gamble that the B-52s would continue to use the same route had paid off – one of the missile battalions that they had moved, the 59th, had shot down two B-52s. In three nights the missile crews had shot down six B-52s over Hanoi and the defenders knew that several more B-52s had crashed in Thailand. The North Vietnamese high command knew that they had defeated the French by causing heavy casualties; now, if they could continue to shoot down large numbers of B-52s and hold out until January when the American Congress returned, victory could well be theirs. It appeared that the North Vietnamese air defenses were about to present their leaders with an "aerial Dien Bien Phu" victory.

For the Americans, the scorecard was sobering. Of the 12 B-52Gs on the third wave that were sent to Kinh No, two were shot down and ten of the 12 crew members were killed. As the last U-Tapao crews came back from the raid, Brigadier General Glenn Sullivan had had enough. "Things were just not going too well. I said that enough is enough, let's make some changes, we've got to get rid of these tactics, so let's get some crew members in here and let's figure out the best way to do this."

At 0930hrs on the 21st, General Sullivan sent SAC a message outlining the necessary changes in tactics.

Brigadier General Glenn Sullivan, the U-Tapao commander, was the man most responsible for the changes in B-52 tactics after Night Four. His outspoken messages to SAC headquarters kept him from being promoted after the war. (Author's collection)

I sent the message to General J. C. Meyer, the commander of SAC, and just sent an information copy to my boss at Eighth Air Force, General Gerald W. Johnson. A lot of people told me this was probably not a very good thing to do, but I wanted to get to where we could get some action, and I didn't want it to have to go through General Johnson and have him say 'I have to check on this' before he sent it to SAC.

Unlike General Sullivan at U-Tapao, Colonel James McCarthy, the commander of the B-52D wing at Andersen, was unwilling to challenge the SAC leadership, saying later: "To have made battlefield modifications [to tactics] any more rapidly than was actually done would have meant doing them on gut reaction or impulse."

The Eighth Air Force staff agreed with General Sullivan. They felt that the B-52s had just been lucky the second night, and that "the separation of the waves … give[s] the [North Vietnamese] an ample chance to deal with 18–21 bombers at a time, instead of all at once, allowing the North Vietnamese to concentrate all their defenses at just one point in the sky." Lower-ranking Eighth staff members called SAC to make that point. SAC listened to the Eighth staff's concerns "politely," as one Eighth staffer remembered, "then equally politely told us to go to hell – no changes, because 'the route was justified because of the targets' orientation [and] avoided or at least minimized exposure to known SAMs sites.'"

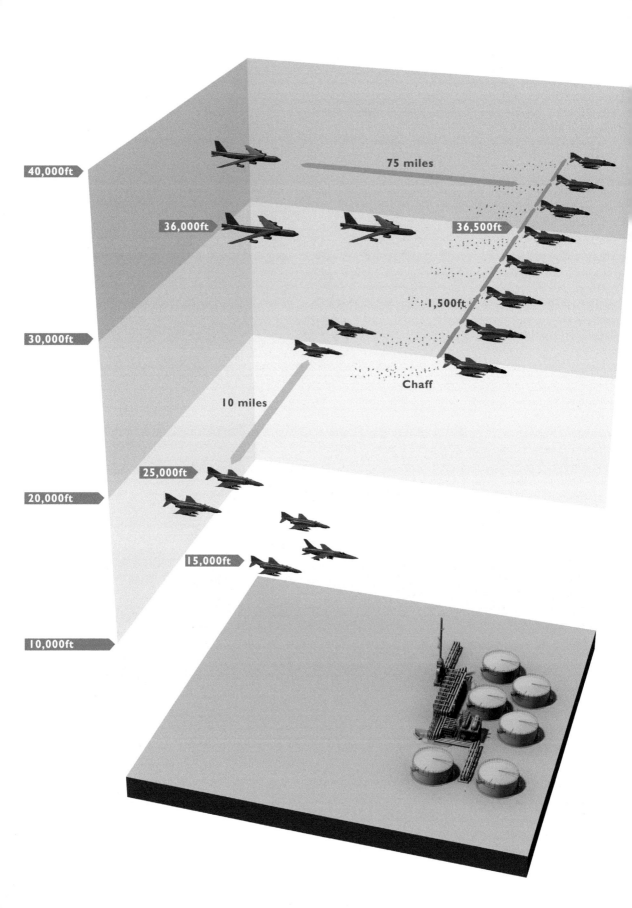

40,000ft

75 miles

36,000ft

36,500ft

1,500ft

30,000ft

Chaff

10 miles

25,000ft

20,000ft

15,000ft

10,000ft

OPPOSITE *LINEBACKER II* MISSION COMPOSITION

For the first four nights, the B-52s flew at the same altitude, 36,000–37,000ft. They were led by eight chaff-dropping F-4s from the 497th Fighter Squadron, 8th Tactical Fighter Wing, Ubon RTAFB, which were at the same altitude or slightly higher than the B-52s. The B-52s tried to fly through the chaff, not above it.

The B-52s had a number of different escorts. There were numerous F-4s flying between 20,000ft and 25,000ft, high enough to be out of the range of antiaircraft fire but low enough that they could keep their speed up to attack MiGs and/or dodge surface-to-air missiles. They flew a "fighting wing" formation with the wingman slightly behind the leader, and about 300ft out. Their random flight patterns were flown roughly parallel to the B-52 track, and would turn toward any MiGs that were detected.

These two-ship formations did not last very long. If a missile was fired at the flight and it had to maneuver, it was impossible for the wingman to stay with the leader. Once they were separated, they continued to patrol single-ship with altitude separation. These escorts came from the 432nd Tactical Reconnaissance Wing at Udorn RTAFB, Thailand, the 8th Tactical Fighter Wing and the 388th Fighter Wing at Korat RTAFB.

The Wild Weasel hunter-killer teams from the 388th Fighter Wing at Korat RTAFB flew in a "wedge" formation, with the F-105G in the lead. They also flew a random course roughly parallel to the B-52s' inbound heading. They flew at 15,000ft – still higher than most antiaircraft fire – because the F-105G was performance-limited and they wanted to be at a lower altitude to improve the performance of the F-105's Standard ARM and Shrike antiradiation missiles.

The Eighth Air Force staff could do nothing more without the support of their leaders, who were unwilling to suggest that the SAC staff were wrong.

By now the North Vietnamese air defense controllers were very familiar with the B-52s' tactics and routes, and this familiarity, the high command hoped, would offset the smaller number of missiles they would have available for the fourth night. But they also realized there would be more air battles over Hanoi, and the Air Defense Command began to rush more missile units to Hanoi from other parts of the country.

By the afternoon of Day Three the 274th's technical battalion, 5th Battalion, had finally arrived in Hanoi and been sent to the warehouse of the 257th Regiment's technical battalion, the 80th, to help them increase the number of assembly lines from three to five. Still, even after they had assembled missiles nonstop for three days, the supply was far below what was needed. One missile man recalled:

> Searching for a missile was like the starving searching for food. As soon as the assembly line completed a missile, a truck was waiting to take it away. In the light of exploding bombs, the new missile was put onto the launcher and within a few minutes was roaring into the sky towards the B-52s. Never before had the 'lives' of the missiles been so short.

The North Vietnamese official history was more measured, but it still showed the urgency of the situation:

> The most pressing technical problem of the campaign was the problem of supplying missiles to the units, and … [a] section was set up with special responsibility for ensuring the supply of missiles and improving both the assembly stage and the distribution stage. But the missile crews were still afraid of running out of missiles. On December 19–20th [Night Two] the number of new missiles the SAM battalions received did not make up for the number of missiles they had fired the first night, so they were not firing as many missiles in a salvo.

This was a special problem, because Soviet tests and combat experience had shown that firing three missiles at a jamming target vastly improved the chances for a hit. Now the North Vietnamese barely had enough missiles to fire two at a target.

Bob Hope on the stage at U-Tapao during *Linebacker II*. This show, one crew member said later, "saved a lot of guys after days of heavy losses." (Author's collection)

The issue remained the lack of assembled missiles. The Hanoi-based technical battalions responsible for assembling the SA-2s had almost doubled the number of assembly lines, but the number of missiles that were coming off the lines was still very small. The SA-2s arrived in North Vietnam packed in a "cigar" storage box that was given to each missile regiment's technical battalion, which was responsible for assembling the missiles, but missile assembly was not a quick or easy process. The main missile and the booster stage were packed separately and had to be removed from their boxes and fueled, the main missile with solid fuel and the booster stage with liquid fuel; this was a delicate, hazardous process that required the crews to be dressed in full protective suits. Next, the missile was filled with the compressed air that powered the control surfaces, then all of the components – warhead, wings, autopilot, warhead, etc – were fitted to the missile. At that point, different frequencies and transponder codes had to be set into each missile's guidance electronics so they would follow only the signals from their designated site's radar, after which the booster section was connected, then the missile went through a final check. On a good day, all the Hanoi technical battalions together could assemble about 40 missiles. Delivery during the night was a problem, and in at least one case missiles were delivered to the wrong battalion.

Night Four: December 21

Faced with the losses of the first three nights, SAC cut the number of B-52s for Night Four, sending only one wave at 0400hrs, 30 Ds from U-Tapao, all of which had the most powerful and sophisticated electronic countermeasures. The North Vietnamese defenders were low on missiles as they waited for the raid at 2000hrs and the raid at 2400hrs, and finally when the raid of 0400hrs appeared they felt free to fire all the missiles they had available.

The Bach Mai airfield was the target for Scarlet cell, the first B-52 cell, but Scarlet 01 had equipment problems and had to move out of formation. On the ground, both the 57th and 78th Missile Battalions watched as a radar return moved away from the formation and four missiles, two from each site, roared up through the overcast and exploded beneath Scarlet 01's right wing. The B-52's wing was engulfed in flames and the bomber began a slow, almost leisurely, roll to the right when the burning wing folded over the top of the aircraft and it plunged towards Hanoi. About four minutes later Blue cell moved in to bomb the same target. Blue 01 had just opened its bomb doors and was beginning to drop its bombs when two SAMs fired by the 93rd Battalion exploded close to the B-52, and the six crew members bailed out. Unfortunately the bombs scattered, and some hit the Bach Mai hospital, killing 28 staff members and giving the North Vietnamese a considerable propaganda victory.

The losses of the third and fourth nights – eight B-52s out of about 120, a loss rate twice what SAC had predicted – sent shock waves through the force. One of the B-52 commanders on Guam admitted later, "if the losses of the third [and fourth] night had continued it would have been prohibitive to continue the operation."

Washington, DC

In Washington, Nixon remained steadfast and was determined to prevail, but determination was not enough. Unless the B-52 losses could be cut – and cut quickly and drastically – his gambit would fail, so after the raids of the fourth night Nixon instructed General Haig to discover why losses were so high. Haig called General Meyer at SAC to find out, and Meyer admitted that they had been using poor tactics and that these were going to change. Haig relayed the information to Nixon, who was furious. Nixon knew that Hanoi would not give in until the B-52s inflicted a high level of damage *at low cost*, and said later:

> [Our] initial heavy losses turned out to be rooted in faulty tactics … the routes flown by the bombers were too predictable. I raised holy hell that they [the B-52s] kept going over the same targets at the same time … [but] finally we got the military to change their [tactics].

Adding to Nixon's problems was the perception that the military did not fully support the operation. Haig said later, "The Pentagon wavered after the early losses… [but] … Nixon told [the Chairman of the Joint Chiefs of Staff, Admiral] Moorer to keep on attacking at full strength or he [Moorer] would be held accountable for the failure."

In Omaha, SAC did not know what to do about the B-52 losses. The members of the SAC's electronic warfare staff had no idea as to how to counter the North Vietnamese missiles, and their distance from the combat zone meant that they were only just beginning to get feedback from the B-52 electronic warfare operators who had flown the first missions.

The SAC staff had to consider another problem: how were the crews handling the losses? Would they be able to stand up under the strain of losing so many people in an unpopular war? SAC could not take the chance of a mutiny, so Hanoi was removed from the target list.

In fact the losses came as a very severe shock to the crews themselves. After years of flying missions with no risk, now, suddenly, many of their friends were gone – a few known to be alive, but most simply down in Hanoi, leaving their comrades with no information about their fate. Additionally, the crews were never told how many aircraft had been actually

When the attacks on Hanoi began, the North Vietnamese had to rush missile units from the south back to Hanoi to reinforce the defenses, as well as send missiles to the capital from Haiphong. (Vietnam News Agency)

shot down and, since Guam aircraft diverted into U-Tapao if they were damaged, rumors abounded of heavy losses At the Anderson clinic the number of people at sick call almost doubled, from 30–40 a day to 55–60.

U-Tapao was blessed with strong leadership, and from the beginning of the operation the 17th Air Division commander, General Glenn Sullivan, and his staff had shown a strong interest in the missions and in the crews' suggestions for improving operations; indeed they knew that General Sullivan had told SAC their tactics were wrong, even though it might cost him his career. Meanwhile, the crews on Guam had the accurate impression that their commanders were not willing to jeopardize their careers by pressing SAC for changes.

After the B-52 losses of the first four nights Seventh Air Force, the tactical force in Vietnam supporting the raid, convened a *Linebacker II* conference to discuss the problems the B-52s were encountering. Though SAC refused to send B-52 crews to such conferences (in fact, most B-52 crews never even knew the conferences took place), one useful thing that did come out was the discovery that the narrow chaff corridors were ineffective and were being blown away by the high-altitude jet stream winds. Now that SAC were sending only one wave of B-52s, the planners at Seventh Air Force decided to concentrate all of their chaff droppers in one area and lay a chaff blanket over the target, rather than hoping that the B-52s could stay in a narrow corridor.

Night Five: December 22

When the word came that U-Tapao would again have to fly all 30 missions into North Vietnam on the fifth night, it seemed that many of the crews – while not ready to mutiny

– were reaching the end of their tether. Fortunately, that fifth afternoon several events came together to alleviate the situation.

The crews learned, to their relief, that they were not going back to Hanoi but heading for the port city of Haiphong. This made an enormous difference, not only because Haiphong was less well defended, but also because the strike was to come in over the Gulf of Tonkin, release its bombs, then turn and exit over the Gulf, spending just a few minutes over land. Seventh Air Force had also decided to try the new chaff tactics discussed earlier that day: two flights of eight F-4s each would fly an elaborate pattern to lay a chaff blanket 30 miles by 12 miles that would drift over Haiphong before the bombers arrived.

The final bit of good news was the arrival of the Bob Hope Christmas show at U-Tapao that afternoon. Hope knew when he arrived that the base had suffered heavy losses and made it a point to take time to meet the crews that were going to be flying the mission that night. The crew members were flattered and very appreciative, and one said later: "it was really grand of [Hope] to take the time to come in and talk to us. He was very sober about it: he didn't tell any funny stories … He just showed his appreciation by taking the time just to come in there and say hello to us." Another B-52 pilot recalled: "The best thing that happened during the … operation to take the pressure off was the Bob Hope show. It saved a lot of guys."

As hoped, Haiphong proved to be a much easier target than Hanoi; and for the first time during *Linebacker II* no B-52 was hit, even though the crews reported a large number of SAMs and two near misses.

Meanwhile, in the White House, Nixon and his advisors received the first reconnaissance photos from the three days of B-52 raids on Hanoi, which clearly showed that many of the targets SAC claimed to have hit had suffered little damage. It was obvious that the B-52s would have to be sent back to Hanoi to inflict more damage if the North Vietnamese were to be forced back to the negotiating table.

Night Six: December 23

On Night Six, SAC moved even further from the North Vietnamese defenses, sending 30 B-52s against a storage area and railroad repair shops close to the village of Lang Dang near the Chinese border. The SAC staff considered Lang Dang a "minor target," but what was important at this point was that there should be no losses, while the B-52s continued to bomb North Vietnam in accordance with the President's desires. Lang Dang was expected to be a classic "milk run," and adding to the crews' confidence were some real changes in the attack plan that reflected the U-Tapao crews' suggestions. The bombers were told to delay their post-target turn to clear the target defenses, then make two small turns rather than one large one and to fly in a significantly larger altitude "block" from 31,000ft to 38,000ft, varying their altitudes as they approached the target, and then changing altitudes again after they dropped their bombs.

At the Seventh Air Force Command Post they were faced with a disaster in the making. The mission plan had arrived late at the fighter and support wings in Thailand, so the support forces were running behind, and to compound the problem there was bad weather in the refueling areas over Laos where the fighters had to refuel prior to their rendezvous with the B-52s. Only the F-111s (which did not need air refueling) were certain to offer full support for the raid. The B-52s might be on their own with no chaffers, fighter escorts or SAM suppression. The Andersen commanders notified SAC about the situation but recommended that the bombers continue on to their targets.

Luck was with them. The raid was well outside of SAM coverage and such raids were allocated to the MiG force. A relatively large number of MiG-21s – at least four – roared off to probe the B-52 force, but the MiGs were cautious and it took some time before they realized they were unopposed. The brunt of their attack was on Topaz and Cooper cells,

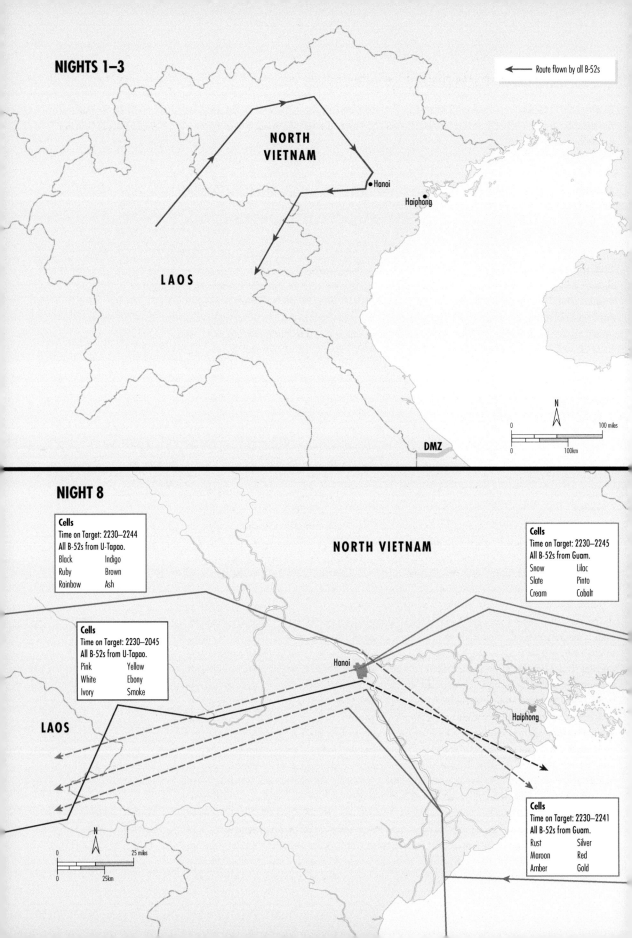

NIGHTS 1–3

NORTH VIETNAM

LAOS

• Hanoi

Haiphong

DMZ

← Route flown by all B-52s

N

0   100 miles
0   100km

NIGHT 8

NORTH VIETNAM

LAOS

Cells
Time on Target: 2230–2244
All B-52s from U-Tapao.
Black   Indigo
Ruby   Brown
Rainbow Ash

Cells
Time on Target: 2230–2045
All B-52s from U-Tapao.
Pink   Yellow
White   Ebony
Ivory   Smoke

Cells
Time on Target: 2230–2245
All B-52s from Guam.
Snow   Lilac
Slate   Pinto
Cream Cobalt

Cells
Time on Target: 2230–2241
All B-52s from Guam.
Rust   Silver
Maroon Red
Amber   Gold

Hanoi

Haiphong

N

0   25 miles
0   25km

During Nights One to Three the B-52 force followed the same route into Hanoi from the northwest, which quickly became predictable. The new routes planned for Night Eight hit Hanoi almost simultaneously from different directions, overwhelming the defenses.

and the MiGs fired four missiles but no bombers were hit. The failed attacks highlighted the MiG-21s' very limited night-intercept capability, even in good conditions, and for one of only a few times in the operation the North Vietnamese did not make the US forces pay for a mistake.

December 24

As part of the Night Six raids, early on December 24 30 B-52s, all flown by U-Tapao crews, bombed the Thai Nyugen railroad yard well away from Hanoi's defenses. Once again Seventh Air Force chaffers laid down a chaff blanket and the B-52s dropped chaff in their small post-target turns to further disrupt the North Vietnamese defenses – a useful tactic but one that had been forbidden by SAC, apparently because the chaff was difficult to load into the B-52.

Although the targets were far from Hanoi's SAM sites, they were still defended, and one B-52, Purple 02, was hit by a 100mm antiaircraft shell that severely damaged some of the B-52's systems. The aircraft commander successfully recovered the B-52 and he and his crew – who had been hit by a SAM on an earlier mission – achieved some notoriety as being the first crew hit twice by North Vietnamese defenses.

Christmas stand-down: Night Seven

President Nixon ordered the Joint Chiefs of Staff to take a 36-hour bombing halt for Christmas, from Christmas Eve until 0600hrs on December 26, Hanoi time. A Christmas cease-fire had been a consistent feature of American operations in Vietnam, and with the domestic pressure against the bombing there was no consideration of continuing the operation. But notwithstanding Christmas parties, the bombing pause generated some bitter reactions from the B-52 crews, who felt that it gave the North Vietnamese an opportunity to continue to reinforce their defenses.

The crews were right, and North Vietnamese Air Defense Command were already using the break in the attacks on Hanoi to improve the capital's defenses. They had concluded that Hanoi would still be the B-52s' main target and expected that the entry and exit routes could be changed, and radar jamming increased. Each day that passed without a raid meant that more missiles were assembled and sent to the missile sites around the capital, and slowly the missile battalions were being brought back to full strength. To counter the expected changes in the B-52 attack patterns, the Air Defense Command began to rearrange their missile battalions, moving some to the northeast and southwest of Hanoi to form a circle around the capital. They also moved in two additional missile battalions from Haiphong, raising the number protecting Hanoi to 13, so that an attack from any direction would now be met by several missile battalions. Missiles had also been called up from Military Region Four, but these had to make their way along difficult roads under the constant threat of air attack and had not arrived.

While the pause helped the North Vietnamese, it also allowed the American staffs both in the combat theater and at SAC to try to solve the problem of the B-52 losses. On the first four nights, the B-52s had made about 300 sorties in the Hanoi defense area and had lost 11 aircraft, a loss rate of about 3.7 percent, with all the losses resulting from bombing targets within 10 miles of the center of the capital. The unmodified Gs had proven to be very vulnerable and after the third night SAC decided that the Gs would not be sent to Hanoi again. Only D models would be used, which had the added benefit of putting more bombs on the important Hanoi targets.

SAC instructed the B-52 electronic warfare officers to change their jamming procedures. However, the missions also showed that jamming protection was seriously degraded when there were only two B-52s in a cell. This was treated with less urgency and, because SAC did not believe the crews could handle changes in tactics, it was said to require "further study."

Analysis also made clear what was brutally obvious to the B-52s crews, that the northwest–southeast route of flight to Hanoi taken in the first four nights was a serious mistake. Despite SAC's insistence that it avoided the bulk of the North Vietnamese defenses, this route carried the B-52s right over the best North Vietnamese SAM regiment, the 261st, which was to score eight of the 15 B-52 kills in the operation.

The Seventh Air Force commander, General John W. Vogt who supplied the tactical support forces, also got into the act and sent a message to the SAC commander:

> Since the beginning of LBII we have made every effort to support B-52 operations … there is inadequate time from receipt of essential SAC information to adequately plan … Often we receive final information on ingress, egress, spacing between cells, etc. after our [orders] should have been disseminated. This severely constrains us in planning optimum tactics and the Wings have inadequate time to prepare for the missions … We must regroup after the brief Xmas standdown … if I am to meet my commitment [to provide] … support for your forces.

Rolling the dice

On December 24, Nixon ordered the Joint Chiefs of Staff to conduct a massive attack on Hanoi on December 26, as soon as the Christmas cease-fire was over, and Admiral Moorer passed the order on to General Meyer at SAC to plan a large mission for that date. The die was cast – the battle would be won or lost on the night of the 26th. If the missions suffered heavy losses, there was no reason to expect the North Vietnamese to return to the peace talks. Congress would convene, cut off money for the war, and South Vietnam and the American POWs would be abandoned. Everything hinged on the mission of December 26.

Still smarting under the criticism of its routes and tactics, when SAC received the order to return to Hanoi they bowed to the inevitable and took themselves out of most of the mission planning. They gave Eighth Air Force general instructions incorporating the lessons of the first four nights, junking the three separate waves spread over eight hours and replacing them with a single attack of 120 B-52s in 15 minutes to overwhelm the defenses and deprive the missile sites of time to reload. One massive support force would assist the attack. Most of the rest of the planning was left to Eighth Air Force, including the precise axis of attack, target routes, and tactics inside the target area, but SAC would still choose the targets. Additionally, SAC supplied the planning data 18 hours before the mission, eliminating most coordination problems. Seventy-eight of the B-52s would come from Andersen, but most of them, 45 Gs, would be sent to targets outside of Hanoi. As usual, U-Tapao did the heavy lifting, sending 42 Ds to the dangerous targets around Hanoi.

The Eighth Air Force plan incorporated many of the changes suggested by the B-52 crews. The B-52s would fly on four basic routes, two raids coming in from Laos and exiting over the Gulf of Tonkin and two raids entering from the Gulf of Tonkin. As the B-52s approached their target area, the raids would split into seven waves to attack ten targets, seven in the Hanoi area, two around Haiphong, and one near Thai Nguyen. Seven of the ten targets would be hit simultaneously by B-52s flying at different altitudes on different axis of attack, and the attack patterns, altitudes, and spacing of each cell would be different from those of the one in front of them. Some of the B-52s' flight paths would actually cross, though with several thousand feet difference in altitude.

Post-target tactics also changed dramatically. After dropping their bombs, the B-52s would change altitude and, except for a few cells, there would be no large post-target turn to blank out the B-52s' jamming antennas over the SAM sites. The whole raid would last only 15 minutes.

The compression of all the B-52s into a single raid allowed Seventh Air Force and the Navy to provide a massive support force of over 110 aircraft for the mission. For the first time, F-111s would attack SAM sites, and the force would have ten Wild Weasel hunter-killer teams to visually attack the missile sites, though the weather was expected to limit their effectiveness.

Twenty-four F-4s would lay a massive, U-shaped chaff blanket over the target areas. With the blanket, the B-52s would not have to worry about staying in a narrow corridor, and the wide dispersion of the chaff complemented the tactic of using multiple attack headings. The compressed target times for the B-52s also solved the problem of the wind blowing the chaff away because on this night the chaff only needed to be in the target area for 15 minutes, instead of the 50 minutes required on the earlier missions.

At the briefing, most of the B-52 crews were elated when they saw the mission routes laid out for them. As the crews came out of the briefing late on the afternoon of the 26th and headed for their aircraft, the word quickly spread around the base at Andersen that this was "the big one," and when the B-52s began to taxi once again a huge crowd was watching.

The spectacle did not disappoint them. Seventy-eight B-52s roared off, and the launch took well over two hours to complete. One observer remembered realizing that what he was seeing "was unique in his lifetime and probably would not be duplicated in the lives of his children." Indeed, what the people at Andersen saw may have been the last mass launch of heavy bombers in history.

On the afternoon of December 26, 78 B-52s were launched *en masse* from Andersen to attack North Vietnam, perhaps the last mass bomber launch in history. (Author's collection)

Red River

Son Tay

2 5

N

6

1

USAF units

B-52 units (all are three-ship cells); accompanied by 432nd TFW (F-4)

1. Black, Ruby, Rainbow, Indigo, Brown, Ash
2. Pink, White, Ivory, Yellow, Ebony, Smoke
3. Snow, Slate, Cream, Lilac, Pinto, Cobalt
4. Rust, Maroon, Amber, Silver, Red, Gold

Supporting units

5. 474th TFW (seven F-111), attacking air bases
6. 497th TFS 9 (16 F-4 chaff bombers), accompani
by 8th TFW (eight chaff escorts)

Other supporting units (not shown)

432nd TFW (20 F-4); B-52 escort)
432nd TRW (18 F-4D/E MiGCAP)
67th TFS (10 F-4C Wild Weasels)
17th WWS (10 F-105G Wild Weasels)
34th TFS (10 F-4E SAM hunter-killers)   5
42nd TEWS (three EB-66)

North Vietnamese Missile Battalion:

These had been relocated and reinforced by the night o
December 26

257th Missile Regiment

A. 57th Missile Battalion
B. 59th Missile Battalion
C. 93d Missile Battalion
D. 94th Missile Battalion

261st Missile Regiment

E. 76th Missile Battalion
F. 77th Missile Battalion
G. 78th Missile Battalion
H. 79 Missile Battalion

274th Missile Regiment

I. 86th Missile Battalion
J. 87th Missile Battalion
K. 88th Missile Battalion
L. 72nd Missile Battalion (on December 26)

VPAF air bases

M. Phuc Yen
N. Hoa Loc
O. Bac Mai

EVENTS   Note: times are Hanoi local time (GMT+7 hours)

1. 2151–2209hrs: 16 F-4s lay a chaff blanket west of Hanoi.

2. 2230hrs: single F-111s strike airfields at Bac Mai, Hoa Loc, and Phuc Yen. Kep (not shown) is also targeted.

3. 2230hrs: nine B-52Ds (cells Snow, Slate, and Cream), 43rd SW, enter from the northeast and strike Hanoi railyards/Gia Lam. Cream 01 and 02 are slightly damaged from a SAM at 2226hrs. Kham Thien Street, a civilian area close to the railyards, is hit causing 400 civilian casualties.

4. 2238hrs: nine B-52Ds (Lilac, Pinto, Cobalt), 43rd SW, enter from the east and strike Hanoi petroleum product storage area/Gia Thong Hanoi.

5. 2232–2246hrs: 15 B-52Ds (Maroon, Amber, Silver, Red from the 43rd SW; Gold from 307th SW) ingress from the Gulf of Tonkin and bomb the Van Dien vehicle depot.

6. 2230–2244hrs: 17 B-52Ds, 307rd SW, enter from west-southwest and bomb Hanoi – Pink, White, Ivory, Yellow, Ebony (01 and 02), and Smoke.

7. 2141hrs: Ebony 02 is hit by two SAMs and downed.

8. 2228–2250hrs: 15 B-52Ds, 307th SW, in six cells (three aircraft ground aborted) ingress from west-northwest and split up. Three cells – Black, Ruby, Rainbow (01 and 02) – bomb the Duc Noi railroad yard from 2228–2235hrs, while cells with seven B-52Ds – Indigo, Brown (01 and 02), and Ash (01 and 02) – bomb the Kinh No complex from 2238–2250hrs.

9. 2248hrs: Ash 01 is hit and badly damaged by a SAM; it returns to U-Tapao and crashes.

Overwhelming force

Night Eight, December 26, 1972

KEY

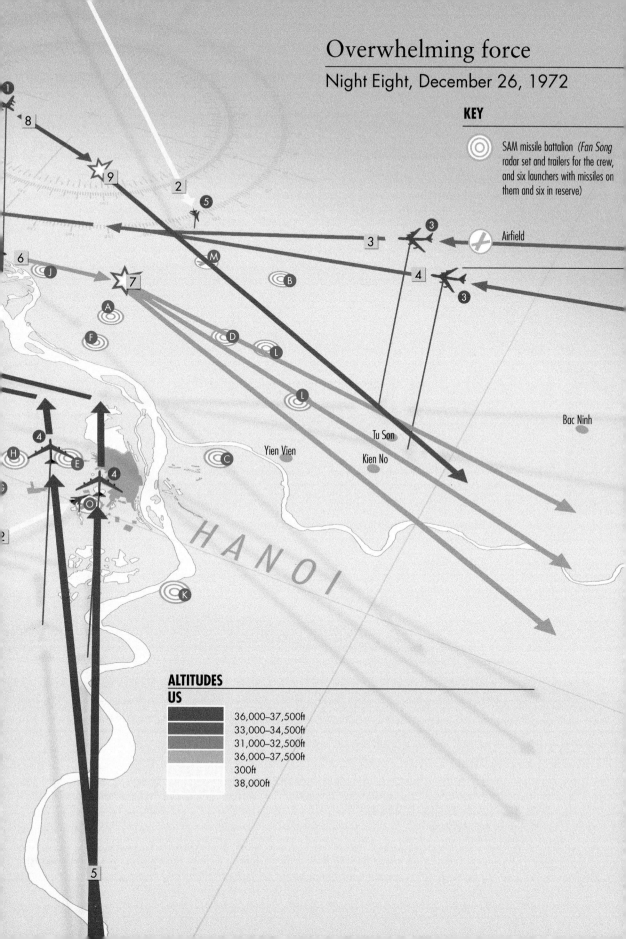

SAM missile battalion (*Fan Song* radar set and trailers for the crew, and six launchers with missiles on them and six in reserve)

Airfield

Bac Ninh

Tu Son

Kien No

Yien Vien

HANOI

ALTITUDES

US

	36,000–37,500ft
	33,000–34,500ft
	31,000–32,500ft
	36,000–37,500ft
	300ft
	38,000ft

LOCATIONS OF B-52 HITS AND LOSSES

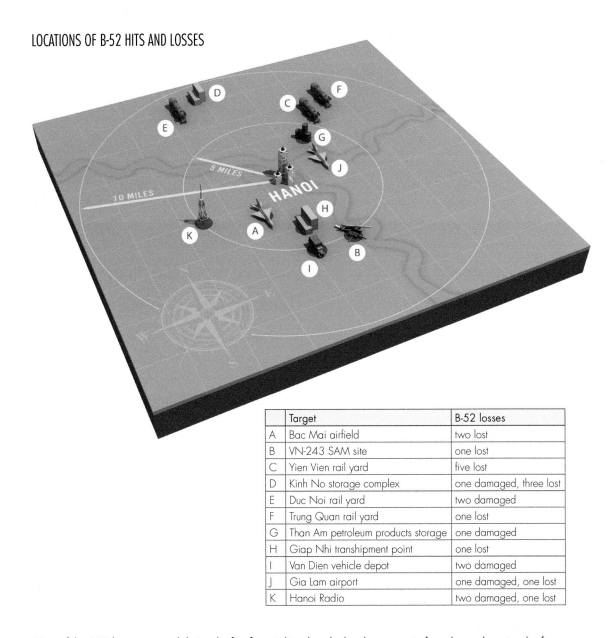

	Target	B-52 losses
A	Bac Mai airfield	two lost
B	VN-243 SAM site	one lost
C	Yien Vien rail yard	five lost
D	Kinh No storage complex	one damaged, three lost
E	Duc Noi rail yard	two damaged
F	Trung Quan rail yard	one lost
G	Than Am petroleum products storage	one damaged
H	Giap Nhi transhipment point	one lost
I	Van Dien vehicle depot	two damaged
J	Gia Lam airport	one damaged, one lost
K	Hanoi Radio	two damaged, one lost

Most of the B-52 losses occurred during the first four nights when the bombers came in from the northwest and, after dropping their bombs, made a post-target turn back to the west. The cluster of hits on B-52s north and northeast of the city is explained by the facts that Kinh No and Yen Vien were important targets and were bombed repeatedly, and that the B-52s' initial routes from the northwest brought the aircraft directly over several SAM sites. When the B-52s attacked these targets in the northeast, they opened their bomb-bay doors as they approached, and this made their radar return much larger, increasing the risk of being hit.

From the third night, the North Vietnamese concentrated more of their Hanoi-based missile units into this area so the B-52s had to fly over heavier defenses. For some – the B-52Gs without the latest electronic jammers – it was possible for the missile radars to overpower, or "burn through," the jamming.

A B-52 that bombed a target in the northeast would then roll into its post-target turn to starboard, which blanked many of its downward-facing jammers. The bomber's post-target turn would last for at least 35 seconds, bringing the aircraft in an arc over the area south or southwest of Hanoi, before it rolled out of its turn and jamming became effective again. The cluster of missile hits south of the city and around to the west was the result.

Meanwhile, U-Tapao's maintenance had been stretched to the limit, and finally began to break. Six bombers aborted on the ground and there were only two spares, so only 38 B-52s from U-Tapao flew the mission. With the aborts the U-Tapao B-52Ds had four cells of two rather than three aircraft, but Eighth opted to do nothing and these two-ship cells – Ash, Rainbow, Brown, and Ebony – headed for Hanoi.

As Ebony 02 climbed out, the number seven engine caught fire. But rather than leave Ebony 01 to fly the mission alone, almost sure suicide without another B-52's jamming support, Ebony 02 pressed on and caught up to Ebony 01 as it turned towards Hanoi.

Even though several new SAM battalions had arrived in Hanoi, the North Vietnamese were concerned:

> We knew that the US … would change their plans for the next wave of action. They would not come from the same direction and would not split into three groups … but send the biggest group of B-52s at the same time … striking straight at Hanoi … the preparations for the attack made the atmosphere at the Air Defense Headquarters quite tense...

Also, though every measure had been taken, the assembly of the missiles still moved with agonizing slowness. On the night of December 26 the Hanoi defenders would have only a little over 100 missiles available, about half the number they had possessed at the start of the campaign.

Night Eight: December 26

Just before 2200hrs on the night of December 26, the North Vietnamese early warning radar crews reported to the Air Defense headquarters that they were picking up the standard US battle pattern unfolding – fighters and Wild Weasels refueling over Laos, EB-66s beginning their jamming, and F-111s crossing the border. Half an hour later 16 F-4s began to lay their chaff blanket just north of Hanoi and after another five minutes eight more F-4s did the same north of Haiphong. The high winds, which had done much to frustrate the corridors on the first seven nights, now blew the corridors together.

What was unfolding was the North Vietnamese defenders' worst nightmare. By the time the B-52s approached, a chaff blanket 40 miles by 23 miles completely covered the Hanoi area and a similar one covered Haiphong. F-111s roared in to attack SAM sites around Hanoi for the first time, while Navy attack aircraft simultaneously began to attack SAM sites around Haiphong.

The North Vietnamese official history described the situation:

> The enemy had altered many of his tactics. They also changed the directions of their bombing and changed the flight paths in and out of the bombing area and they began collectively and unceasingly bombing a lot of targets at the same time within a short period … The initial situation was very complicated. There was much radar jamming and 'fake B-52s' [the chaff corridor] as well as squads of [Wild Weasels] continuously launching guided [anti-radiation] missiles. The enemy sent many groups of B-52s into the area simultaneously, all of the groups arrived at their bombing targets at the same time [and] this simultaneous attack from many directions caused us many difficulties in focusing our firepower, so we were not able to fire at all of them in time. The enemy split into many groups and while there were many tight formations they did not stay in the range of our missiles for long.

The Air Defense headquarters was badly overwhelmed and as the early warning system broke down, the SAM battalions had to use their own *Fan Song* radars to search for targets, a technique that not only was inefficient but also vastly increased their vulnerability to anti-

INTI

Damage on the Kinh No complex. It was one of the most heavily bombed targets of *Linebacker II,* but in the process three B-52s were shot down and another damaged. (Author's collection)

radiation missiles. The heavy chaff blanket also forced the missile crews to abandon their automatic tracking and fall back on the less efficient three-point manual tracking of the missiles all the way to the target.

As the North Vietnamese missile crews tried to cope with the new situation, six B-52 cells attacked the Giap Nhi railroad yard from the south, exactly the opposite of the direction that they had attacked Hanoi previously. The six cells then split into two groups, one of two cells and the other of four, and the groups attacked from different directions.

Unfortunately, two of the cells had only two B-52s and the new tactics were negated to some extent by their limited jamming. Ebony was one of the two-ship cells, and Ebony 02 was approaching the target when it was tracked by both the 76th and 78th Battalions of the 257th Regiment. Each battalion fired two missiles and manually tracked the B-52 as it approached. The first 76th missile narrowly missed, but the second of the missiles exploded in front of the B-52. A few seconds later a missile from the 78th hit the left wing and a brilliant flash lit up the sky as the bomber blew up in midair, and large pieces fell burning to the ground. There were a few seconds of stunned silence among the American forces. Then, "miraculously," as one crew member recalled, emergency beepers from the parachutes began to sound. Four Ebony 02 crew members survived and were captured.

For the sixth time the B-52s attacked Kinh No, whose defenses had already brought down three of the bombers. Two of the three cells going against Kinh No had only two B-52s in each cell, and with limited jamming coverage the defenses again scored. Ash 01 was hit on the right side by a missile from 86th Battalion of the 274th Regiment; the badly damaged B-52 made it back to Thailand but crashed trying to land at U-Tapao.

Even with two losses, the Night Eight raid was a tremendous success. In 22 minutes the B-52s dropped over 2,000 tons of bombs and all indications were that the North Vietnamese defenses had been completely overwhelmed. The two B-52s lost had been in two-ship cells, and that would have to be changed, but the small post-target turn appeared to be effective,

changing the B-52s' flight path and altitude to make it more difficult for the SA-2 guidance officers to manually track the aircraft and keeping the B-52s from blanking their own jamming. In addition to the changes in the routes and post-target turns, a good deal of the credit for the low loss rate must be given to the large, dense chaff cloud over the area that protected most of the flights. On Night Eight 85 percent of the B-52s were inside the chaff cloud as opposed to 5 percent on earlier missions, and the North Vietnamese noted the enormous increase in "fake B-52s."

SAC's fear of collisions, which had led it to stereotyped routes instead of tactical maneuvering, proved to be misplaced. The altitude separation was effective, and even though many cells missed their time over target badly (two were at least three minutes off their time and 20 miles off course) and the flight paths crossed, there were no near misses between B-52s.

Unfortunately, there was also some serious collateral damage. An errant string of bombs fell on a shopping district on Kham Thien street and killed over 250 civilians. This accident was significantly different from the damage to the Bach Mai hospital, which had been caused when a B-52 was hit by a SAM as it dropped its bombs, and Gia Lam, which had been bombed deliberately in violation of orders. The damage to Kham Thien street was caused because the B-52s' bombing system simply had a large margin of error, and this street fell on the very edge of that margin.

The successful bombing and low losses on Night Eight apparently changed the North Vietnamese political calculations, and the next day they sent a message to the United States offering to restart negotiations in Paris on January 8. Nixon replied that he wanted the

The costliest target during *Linebacker II* was the Yen Vien railroad yard, where five B-52s were shot down; but the yard was for practical purposes wiped out. (Author's collection)

Ebony 02 blowing up over Hanoi during the mass raid of December 26. Two crew members escaped. (Vietnam News Agency)

negotiations to begin on January 2 and that Kissinger should go to Paris on January 8. To reinforce his message to both the North Vietnamese and the South Vietnamese, he let the B-52s continue bombing.

Night Nine: December 27

On December 27, just after Nixon sent his message, 60 B-52s and their support aircraft attacked with a new wrinkle – for the first time the B-52s were going to bomb SAM sites. Ash cell was scheduled to bomb one of the SAM sites, VN-243. Another cell was assigned to bomb SAM site VN-549, the "killer site" which US intelligence identified (wrongly) as that which had already shot down six B-52s. The B-52s would use essentially the same tactics they had used on Night Eight – multiple entry headings, a chaff blanket, moderate and varied post-target turns, and large altitude separations.

But the North Vietnamese defenses still had teeth. As the B-52s moved in to attack, the 72nd Battalion, newly arrived from Haiphong, picked up Cobalt cell, the first cell of B-52s. The *Fan Song* burned through the jamming and when the radar return became clear the 72nd fired two missiles at Cobalt 01, hitting it and turning it into a flaming torch. Cobalt 01 was the last B-52 lost over Hanoi.

At about the same time Ash cell was attacking a SAM site. For some reason, after bomb release Ash 02 rolled into a steep evasive maneuver that put the aircraft well away from the mutual jamming support of the other B-52s of the cell. It was hit by a SAM but escaped and crashed in Thailand.

Even though only two B-52s had been lost, the ferocity of the North Vietnamese defenses surprised and disturbed the American commanders and dispelled any feeling that the battle was over. The US crews reported that the North Vietnamese had fired about 90 missiles that night, more missiles per sortie than they had fired on any other raid, and some of the crews said it was "the worst night" they had experienced.

The number of SAMs fired and the losses of December 27 raised questions about the advisability of continuing the B-52 attacks, and General Clay, the Commander of the Pacific Air Force (CINCPACAF), sent a message to Washington saying, "it seems to me that there are few if any targets remaining in [North Vietnam] which are worth the continuing [B-52] losses we are experiencing." Once again, this message was not received kindly in Washington, where the White House believed that the military was beginning to be affected by the negative publicity from the raids.

But while the SAMs were causing considerable angst among American intelligence and the B-52 crews, the North Vietnamese were in fact in deep trouble, and now the game was up. Though there was still a large number of missiles in containers, the North Vietnamese simply could not assemble them fast enough, and the new American tactics and the massive chaff corridors were overwhelming the defenses. Desperate, the North Vietnamese now ordered their MiG-21s to take part in the operation to offset the small number of SA-2s. By dawn on December 28, though neither side realized it, the battle was over.

Night Ten: December 28

On Night Ten 60 more B-52s were sent to North Vietnam without loss and only a few SAMs were reported. It marked the "tipping point." The North Vietnamese defenses were deteriorating. After this mission, the B-52 crews were full of confidence, and one summed up their feelings: "... we went 4 miles from Hanoi and it was a piece of cake … we were sure that the North Vietnamese were running out of SAMs."

While more MiGs came up, they did not help. A MiG-21 flown by Vu Xuan Thieu pressed an attack against the B-52s, but before he was able to get close Thieu was shot down by two prowling F-4s. The North Vietnamese later claimed that Thieu's MiG collided with the B-52 and both crashed, but no B-52s were lost that night.

Night Eleven: December 29

On December 29, Night Eleven, the B-52s moved away from the center of the still heavily defended capital. Sixty B-52s attacked SAM storage areas at the Lang Dang railroad yard. Once again there were no losses and only a few SAMs were reported. After two straight nights of bombing without a loss, one B-52 crew member spoke for the entire force when he said, "there was no threat. It was easy pickings."

The North Vietnamese saw the same thing and relayed this to Washington with an offer to return to the Paris talks for "technical discussions" on 2 January. President Nixon agreed and gave the order to suspend bombing north of the 20th Parallel. The last raid of B-52s were airborne and heading for their targets when the order was flashed to all the US bases that *Linebacker II* was to end at 0659hrs, December 30, Hanoi time. About two hours after Eighth Air Force received the orders, at 2345hrs, Grey 03, the last B-52 in the last wave, dropped its bomb load on Trai Ca and returned safely to base. *Linebacker II* was over.

On the afternoon of December 31, General Sullivan received a message from Bob Hope:

How happy we were to hear the news of a bombing halt. You and your men can take a well-deserved bow for your great contribution to any peace we get. May you have the biggest 73 ever, and that goes for all in your command.

AFTERMATH AND ANALYSIS

Losses

Ten B-52s had been shot down over North Vietnam and five others were seriously damaged and crashed in Laos or Thailand. Thirty-three B-52 crew members were killed or missing in action, another 33 became prisoners of war, and 26 more were rescued. All the B-52 losses were to SA-2s. Two F-111s were shot down; one of these was lost to small arms and the other simply disappeared.

North Vietnamese air defense forces claimed that 34 B-52s and four F-111s had been shot down during the campaign, but the losses admitted by the United States can be confirmed by the names of the crew members, while the claims of the North Vietnamese cannot. The North Vietnamese claim 17 B-52s shot down "on the spot," which meant they actually found the wreckage. This is much more reasonable, since B-52s were large and when blown up they might fall in several large pieces.

The North Vietnamese government reported 1,624 civilians killed by the bombing, and many more injured.

The United States claimed that 483 SA-2s had been fired at the B-52s. The North Vietnamese state that they fired 266, certainly the more accurate figure.

In the course of *Linebacker II* 729 B-52s dropped over 15,000 tons of bombs on North Vietnam. There is no question that the B-52s were a devastating weapon, and the pictures on pages 82 and 83 show just a few of their targets. Viewing these and realizing that by the end of *Linebacker II* B-52s were roaming over all of North Vietnam without opposition makes it easy to understand why the North Vietnamese returned to the negotiating table. It is also worth noting that the United States was able to continue B-52 strikes against North Vietnamese forces in South Vietnam during the latter part of *Linebacker II*.

The end of the war

While still publicly defiant, the North Vietnamese seemed to believe that their military and political options were gone. They had seen their Soviet and Chinese allies issue

Le Duc Tho, North Vietnam's senior negotiator in Paris, and US National Security Advisor Henry Kissinger after signing the peace agreement on January 23, 1973. Tho later declined the Nobel Peace Prize. (Photo by Daily Express/ Archive Photos/Getty Images)

pro forma denunciations of the bombings but take no substantive actions, and without their support there was little prospect of the North Vietnamese continuing. On January 3, Hanoi announced that both sides had resumed their meetings in Paris the day before, and that Le Duc Tho had left for Paris to meet with Kissinger.

Before Kissinger left for Paris, he and Nixon met with Secretary of State Rodgers, Secretary of Defense Laird, and Admiral Moorer to review the situation and to ensure that there would be no leaks of information while the delicate negations were under way. Kissinger also warned the military not to claim victory or anything else that might keep the North Vietnamese from signing the agreement, and the Defense Department sent a worldwide message to all military commanders telling them:

> There must be no, repeat no, comment of any sort whatsoever from any DOD personnel, civilian or military, of whatever rank … There is to be no comment, no speculation, no elaboration, and no discussion about the White House announcement [about the suspension of the bombing and resumption of negotiations].

Kissinger and Tho's initial Paris meeting was "frosty at the outset but thawed during the course of the meeting," and, while Kissinger was pleased to find that the North Vietnamese

The North Vietnamese consider *Linebacker II* a major victory, naming it the "Dien Bien Phu in the skies," and regularly celebrate it. Here is one of the signs from the 45th anniversary in December 2017. (Author's collection)

protests about the bombing were "brief and relatively mild," he left the meeting without a real feel for the situation. In a message to Nixon he noted that it would be difficult for the North Vietnamese to give in on the issues in the first meeting after the intense bombing, and cautioned that "they [may] plan to stonewall us again."

Then, the next day, Kissinger said he was upbeat at the "mood and businesslike approach" and told Nixon, "We celebrated the President's birthday today by making a breakthrough on the negations," while cautioning that "the Vietnamese have broken our hearts before."

To Kissinger's dismay the information was leaked and he blew up, and insisted that his information be confined to the President alone, telling his staff:

> [I]f our geniuses [in Washington] want to blow up the agreement they have hit on the perfect formula to do so … there must not be the slightest hint of the present status to the bureaucracy, cabinet members, the congress, or anyone else … What has brought us to this point is the President's firmness and the North Vietnamese belief that he will not be affected by either Congressional or public pressure. Le Duc Tho has repeatedly made these points to me, so it is essential that we keep our fierce posture during the coming days. The slightest hint of eagerness could prove suicidal.

Things now moved swiftly and by January 11 the negotiations were far enough along for Kissinger to be concerned with events in Saigon and eager to avoid a repeat of Thieu's performance in late October. He told Nixon:

> It must be clearly understood that when we conclude here we must proceed to an initialing whatever Thieu's answer is. Under no circumstances will Hanoi hold still for a repetition of October or a renegotiation without blowing the whole agreement. We cannot get any more concessions.

Nixon understood the issue well. Earlier, on January 5, Nixon had tried to placate Thieu with assurance of continued assistance in the post-settlement period, and on January 14 he took a tougher line and told President Thieu, "I have therefore irrevocably decided to proceed to initial the agreement on 23 January 1973 … I will do so, if necessary, alone."

At the same time he sent General Alexander Haig to Saigon to talk to Thieu, and on January 16, Haig reiterated Nixon's message: that the United States would guarantee South Vietnam's security if Thieu would sign the peace agreement, but that the United States would sign the agreement under any circumstances. If South Vietnam refused to sign it when Congress returned, it would mean an almost certain cut-off of funds to South Vietnam. On January 20, Thieu agreed to sign.

It was over. After considerable technical haggling, on January 23 Kissinger and Tho initialed the agreement and, on January 27, the United States, North Vietnam, South Vietnam, and the Viet Cong signed it. American POWs were returned and America's military involvement in Vietnam was over.

Linebacker II: the North Vietnamese view

The North Vietnamese – now the Vietnamese – have a simple view of the operation, best summed up by the name they have given the battle – the "Dien Bien Phu in the skies." The battle has a place in Vietnamese history as the victory that drove the Americans out, a major step on the way to unifying their country, and the Vietnamese now place it on the same level as the battle of Dien Bien Phu, the battle that forced the French from Indochina.

There is something to be said for the Vietnamese view that they won a victory in that December. After *Linebacker II*, the United States left Vietnam, much as the French left after their defeat at Dien Bien Phu. With the Americans gone, the North Vietnamese were able to use the troops left in South Vietnam as a framework for building up their forces. In April 1975, these North Vietnamese forces swept through South Vietnam and completed their goal of unifying the country.

Beyond its real significance and the parallels to the land battle of Dien Bien Phu, there is also a psychological reason that the "Dien Bien Phu in the skies" has a place in the ranks of historic Vietnamese victories. The battle was not fought by an army on some distant battlefield; instead, it was a major battle that took place in the capital, and a battle where a large number of the civilian population was involved. Certainly, everyone in North Vietnam at that time knew someone who was touched by the bombing, and this massive participation in the battle unified the country and has enhanced its value as a symbol of Vietnam's defeat of the United States.

Linebacker II: the American view

On the American side, the withdrawal was inevitable, and it had been decided the previous May that the North Vietnamese forces were going to stay in South Vietnam. The battle was an important victory but equally a symbol, a point in time that marked the end of American participation in the war.

Linebacker II persuaded the North Vietnamese to sign a peace agreement that they had rejected in December, an agreement that obtained the release of the American POWs, and got the best deal possible for South Vietnam given US domestic realities.

The Nixon/Kissinger/Haig calculation of the effect of the B-52 raids was correct. While the North Vietnamese air defenders fought well, there is considerable evidence that the raids deeply affected the population and the leadership. The B-52 bombings *were* profoundly different. The POWs reported that their guards were stunned and frightened, and more importantly the North Vietnamese official press reports and writings after the operation reflect the same view. But this does not mean that continued B-52 bombing might have

US prisoners of war on their way back to the United States. (USAF)

brought further concessions from the leadership. There is a long distance from frightening the population to forcing strong-willed government leaders into some form of concrete action against their national interests.

It also does not seem unreasonable to say that *Linebacker II* might have succeeded in its aim of preserving South Vietnam. There seems to be no question that the B-52 bombing of Hanoi and the terrific casualties that North Vietnamese forces suffered from US air attacks from April to October 1972 intimidated the North Vietnamese leadership. Had Nixon had remained in power and the United States kept a significant B-52 presence in Asia, it is doubtful that the North Vietnamese would have tried a conventional invasion of South Vietnam. It was only after an external event – the fall of Nixon because of Watergate – that the fall of South Vietnam began to seem likely, if not inevitable.

During the operation the United States was well served by its leadership at both the top and bottom. The President, encouraged by Haig and Kissinger, was decisive and avoided interfering with the military operation. At the bottom, the B-52 crews and their support forces fought courageously and well, and most of the leaders and staffs in the combat zone, with one notable exception, from Eighth Air Force down, provided strong support and leadership.

Where the US performance faltered was at the middle level – at the Department of Defense and Joint Chiefs of Staff, but most specifically at the top levels of the Strategic Air Command. It is reasonable to say the United States could have actually lost the battle because of the SAC's failings. The heavy losses, which frightened the SAC leadership so much that they were unwilling to press the attack when North Vietnam was almost out of missiles, gave the North Vietnamese real confidence that they could win a victory, and that was reflected in their pre-Christmas unwillingness to return to peace talks.

What if …?

If *Linebacker II* has a strong symbolic significance for the Vietnamese as the "Dien Bien Phu in the skies," it also has a strong symbolic position in parts of the American military as "what might have been." It is an article of faith among some former US military officers that the Vietnam War was lost because the US political leadership used half measures until late in 1972. When it finally unleashed its full military capability – symbolized by *Linebacker II* – the North Vietnamese quickly surrendered. The question that constantly arises when discussing *Linebacker II* is, "Why didn't the United States do this sooner?" or, more often, it arises as the statement, "If the United States had used the B-52s on Hanoi sooner, the war could have been won."

But is this reasonable? Could the United States have used massive force – specifically, the B-52s – earlier to "win the war," that is, to force the North Vietnamese to give up their aim of uniting the country?

The answer to this question requires a broad world view that considers at a minimum not just US military capabilities but the international situation, US internal considerations, the North Vietnamese leadership and their willpower, and the dynamics of the Cold War at the time.

Taking this broader view, on the US side it is important to note that at no point in the war did the military think that a *Linebacker II*-type campaign was necessary. While most senior military officers believed that a heavy bombing campaign would dramatically shorten the war and cut US casualties, none thought it was critical to winning the war. The US military believed that the United States was already winning the war, albeit slowly. The thought that the US might lose the war was ludicrous, and as long as the American military continued to believe that the United States was winning the war it would have been difficult – perhaps impossible – to justify a bombing campaign on the scale of *Linebacker II*. Later it would have been totally impossible in the light of the burgeoning, increasingly aggressive anti-war movement.

Another consideration is that while the Cold War was in full swing the B-52s were absolutely necessary as part of America's nuclear deterrent and thus less expendable in a minor war. Certainly, the SAC would have objected vociferously to the possibility of losing precious B-52s in a war that the US was already winning.

Additionally, in the context of the Cold War, a *Linebacker II*-type bombing campaign might have brought increased Soviet and Chinese aid or even intervention. While the idea of such intention has been discredited today, it was a real – and more than that, legitimate – concern for US policy makers at the time. To ignore the possibility would have been irresponsible.

Had the United States started the bombing much earlier, on the North Vietnamese side the power of Ho Chi Minh's personality would have prevented the North Vietnamese from giving up their ambition to unite the country. The idea that bombing could have cowed Ho borders on being ridiculous; one thing that World War II demonstrated is that populations and leaders are resilient to bombing, and there is no reason to believe that Ho and the North Vietnamese were any different. That, combined with the fact that the North Vietnamese had relatively little infrastructure to destroy, suggests that massive bombing would not have broken the North Vietnamese will.

Is it possible that Ho's death might have weakened the North Vietnamese determination to the extent that the B-52 raids could have broken it? This seems unlikely. The leadership certainly had the same objective as Ho, to unify the country and remove the foreigners, and giving up Ho's aims would have destroyed their legitimacy.

By the time Nixon was elected the possibility of effective Soviet intervention in the event of a massive air campaign had arguably increased. Prior to 1969 the main Soviet export surface-to-air missile system was the SA-2, but by 1969 the Russians had shown a willingness to provide a

The B-52 Victory Museum in Hanoi has a large number of artifacts celebrating the "Dien Bien Phu in the skies" victory, including this B-52 pieced together from wreckage. (Author's collection)

new SAM system, the SA-3 *Goa*, to their allies. As long as the Soviets and the United States were at odds, a *Linebacker II*-type bombing campaign might have encouraged the Soviets to supply SA-3s to the North Vietnamese, and SA-3s would have exponentially increased B-52 losses. It was not until Kissinger and Nixon had developed their relationship with the Soviets that it became unlikely that they would provide SA-3s to North Vietnam, and in the end they did not.

There is a second counterfactual that should be examined – once *Linebacker II* started, could the United States have continued the bombing until it forced major concessions from the North Vietnamese, specifically the removal of their troops from South Vietnam?

The answer is almost certainly no. While General Alexander Haig is one of the many who believes that a longer period of B-52 bombing would have forced further concessions, he also believes that at that point the war was already settled – the aim of the bombing was never to return to the *status quo ante* May 1972. The reason was simply a matter of political support.

A more interesting question is as follows: if the raids had been executed properly from the beginning, could the United States have forced movement in the few days allotted? If one believes that more B-52 bombing would have forced the North Vietnamese to more concessions, it is worth pondering what the North Vietnamese Politburo would have done if they had run out of missiles and the B-52s had been able to pound Hanoi unopposed from December 21.

Another point to consider is whether the bombing could have failed, and if so what would have happened. SAC's planning failures meant that the battle came close to ending in an incredible, almost inconceivable, disaster. The losses of the third night, and the failure of nerve in Omaha that allowed the North Vietnamese to resupply their missile units, gave North Vietnam the confidence it needed to hold out long enough to let Congress cut off funds for the war. Had SAC not turned the planning over to Eighth Air Force, and if the United States had suffered a large number of B-52 losses the night of December 26, it is difficult to see how the B-52 attacks could have continued. If *Linebacker II* had failed, there is no doubt that at that point the United States Congress would have terminated all funding for the war. The results of such a cut-off are clear: the withdrawal of American forces, the quick loss of South Vietnam, a huge blow to American prestige in the region with unforeseen consequences in Thailand and the rest of Asia, and the North Vietnamese left with over 600 American prisoners of war to use as negotiating pawns and to generate further humiliation. For those who think that the United States lost the war, this alternative scenario is worth pondering – it would have been a *real* loss.

SELECT BIBLIOGRAPHY

Primary sources

Sources in this section are available at: Air Force Historical Research Agency (AFHRA), 600 Chennault Circle, Maxwell AFB, AL 36122-6424, USA

ARC LIGHT Compression Tactics, message sent from General Sullivan to General Johnson, 22/0806Z Dec 72.

Annex to the History of Eight Air Force, 1 July 1972–30 June 1973, Chapter V, Linebacker II

Chaff Effectiveness in Support of Linebacker II Operations, Briefing for the SAC Director of Operations, undated (probably mid-1973)

History of Seventh Air Force, July 1972–19 March 1973, Volume 1

History of the 307th Strategic Wing, October–December 1972, Volume 1

History of the 388th Tactical Fighter Wing, Korat RTAFB, October–December 1972, Volume 1

History of Eighth Air Force, 1 July 1972–30 June 1973, Volumes I and II, 23 August 1974

History of the 43rd Strat Wing, July 72–31 Dec 72

LB II Air Operations Survey

Linebacker Operations September–December 1972, Project CHECO Southeast Asia Report, 31 December 1978

Linebacker II Operational Reports, 2 July 1973, J35 Memo 0083-73

Linebacker II USAF Bombing Survey, April 1973

Operations Analysis: Linebacker II, Air Operations Study Ground Presented to CINCPACAF, January 18, 1973

SAC Operations in Linebacker II, Tactics and Analysis

Seventh Air Force History, Summer 72–Dec 72, Volume IV

Taking Aim at the B-52s, General Hoang Van Khanh; *Nahn Dan* (official Vietnamese government newspaper), 6–10 December 1982, translated by Linh Cuu My, Vietnam Magazine, *Tactical Air Command SEA Tactics Review Brochure*, Volume 1, January 1973

Tactical Air Command SEA Tactics Review Brochure, Volume II, April 1973,

USAF Air Operations in Southeast Asia, 1 July 1972–15 August 1973, CORONA HARVEST: Volume V

USAF Air Operations in Southeast Asia 1 July 1972–15 August 1973, Volume 1, Headquarters PACAF, undated

Secondary sources

Eschmann, Karl J., *Linebacker; The Untold Story of the Air Raids Over North Vietnam*, Ivy Books (Ballentine), 1989

Grosshuesch, L.V., Director, Operations Plans, DCS/Operations, PACAF, *Summary and Analysis of Linebacker II*, 1 February 1973,

Heitz, Martin F. and Rider, Leslie, *The Prestige Press and the Christmas Bombing, 1972*, The Ethics and Public Policy Center, 1980

Hopkins, Charles K., *SAC Bomber Operations in the Southeast Asia War*, Volume IV, Strategic Air Command SAC Historical Monograph #204

Hopkins, William, *Linebacker II Chronology*, no date, probably mid-1973

Kissinger, Henry, *White House Years*, Phoenix Press, 2000

Luu Trong Lan, *Christmas Bombing: Dien Bien Phu in the Air,* QOND, Ha Noi, Vietnam

McCarthy, Brigadier General James R., *Linebacker II: A View From the Rock*, Office of Air Force History, 1985

Nalty, Bernard C., *Tactics and Techniques of Electronic Warfare; Electronic Countermeasures in the Air War against North Vietnam 1965–1973,* Defense Lion, 2013

Pape, Robert A., *Bombing to Win: Air Power and Coercion in War*, Cornell University Press, Ithaca, NY, 1996

Peterson, Maxie J., Captain, USAF, *Linebacker II Air Operations Summary (18–29 December 1972)*, Operations Analysis Office, Headquarters PACAF, March 1973

Thompson, Wayne, *Rebound: The Air War Over North Vietnam 1966–1973* (July 1997 draft), Air Force History and Museums Program

Vassiliev, Alexei, *Missiles Over the Lotus Flower*, unpublished work (author is Director of the Institute of African and Arab Studies, Russian Academy Sciences, Moscow)

Interviews

Interview with Jerry Sowell, SA-2 Engineer Eglin AFB Florida, December 17, 1999

Interviews with General Alexander Haig, October 1998–August 1999

Interview with Brigadier General McCarthy, AF Oral History Project, June 1973

INDEX